Germania, U.S.A.

GERMANIA, U.S.A.

¶ Social Change in New Ulm, Minnesota

by NOEL IVERSON

The University of Minnesota Press
MINNEAPOLIS

PREFACE

AMERICAN sociologists have turned most often toward an interpretation of their own society — from Park's pioneer studies of the American city to the broad, searching portrayals of the character, organization, and drift of American society as seen in the works of Hans Gerth and C. Wright Mills, David Riesman, William H. Whyte, Jr., and numerous others. Many have sought to explain the emergence and transformation of the social forms and structures that constitute their contemporary society. Chief among the subforms of American society are ethnic and status communities. They have long figured importantly in the work of American sociologists. This book is a continuation of this interest.

This study branches off somewhat, however, from the mainstream of American community studies, represented by the Middletown–Yankee City series. *Germania, U.S.A.* presents a fusion of ethnic and status community analysis while at the same time it attempts to sharpen the distinction between class and status. It also departs from the usual study of the ethnic community in America in two respects: Germania (New Ulm, Minnesota) was founded in the countryside by a group of comparatively highly placed immigrants (most ethnic communities grew up in large cities and comprised low-placed foreigners); Germania's founders soon re-formed into an upper status subcommunity (the assimilation of an ethnic community has usually led to its dissolution; the formation of a status community is an unusual outcome of assimilation).

66878

American society has integrated its institutions and attained consistency in its mores at the expense of its subcommunities. In the consolidation of wealth, status, and power that has characterized the emergence of the American mass society, all subcommunity forms have been accommodated in one way or another. Two general processes of accommodation, exemplified in this book, are the assimilation of ethnic minorities and the formation of status communities.

The former, a process of subcultural disintegration, tends to unite immigrant minorities with the native majority, whereas the latter tends to separate native status equals from the majority. Conceivably, ethnic assimilation to the wider society may be a prelude to the formation of a status community; when the two processes are joined in this manner, special advantages over the normal pattern of assimilation to American life are secured. These advantages are seen in the linkage of wealth, prestige, and influence in the status community. Its monopoly on access to these values gives the status community a persistency not ordinarily enjoyed by an ethnic community. The Turners of Germania testify to the advantages of status community formation: their accommodation to American life has been highly successful.

The Turners are descendants of German immigrants who came to America during the political and economic upheaval accompanying the revolutions of 1830 and 1848. Some formed colonization societies and pushed westward to the Mississippi in search of cheap land. In 1856, a group of Turners founded Germania, U.S.A., deep in Minnesota Territory, hoping to achieve the political and religious freedom and the economic security denied them in their fatherland. Hence Germania is the product of nineteenth-century forces far removed from the realities of life on the American frontier. Who could have imagined that the whirlpool of romantic idealism and nationalism which had drawn together German utopian aspirations of unity and folkic identity would cast up on American shores yet another experiment in frontier socialism? Germania was such a venture.

Physically removed as they were from the majority–minority

tensions of the urban milieu in which immigrants usually found themselves, the Germania Turners were afforded the luxury of working out their adaptation to American life at a leisurely pace and in their own way. Having financed the settlement of Germania, they naturally gravitated toward positions of civic and cultural leadership in the community, a rare experience for immigrants. Moreover, they soon won recognition from the townspeople as status superiors. Their leadership extended to assimilation itself, the Turners accommodating themselves to the majority American culture with greater ease and speed than the non-Turners of Germania. Thus, significantly, the common immigrant experience of acute cultural marginality is virtually unknown among the Germania Turners. Moreover, generational conflict of identity gave them little cause for concern; Germania's marginal men were second-generation descendants of non-Turner immigrants who struggled to reconcile the disparities between two worlds. First-generation Turners, by contrast, repudiated their Old World origin as a matter of policy.

My intention is to show why the Turners founded Germania as an ethnic community in the first place and then proceeded to consolidate their forces (they were numerically in the minority within a short time), emerging as the top status group of the community. Though uncommon, this situation is not unique. It illustrates a general principle about the conditions under which an ethnic community will fail to maintain its original form: "Whenever the ethnic alien is of as high or higher class and status derivation as the group among whom he has settled, he tends to form into status communities rather than into ethnic communities."

The historical peculiarities of the Turners account for their founding an ethnic community. Their subsequent appearance as a prominent status group in Germania is to be understood by means of the theory of community formation supplied by Don Martindale in *American Social Structure*. Four aspects of change — class, status, power, and assimilation — are covered in this book. Each aspect is viewed according to differences between two generations of Germania's upper status group, the Turners, and two corresponding generations of non-Turners.

Many people have lent their encouragement, their time and labor, their suggestions and their sympathy to this study. It would not have succeeded without them. To all I am grateful, even though I express my indebtedness to only a few: at the University of Minnesota, Professor Don Martindale, who always brought clarity and radiated confidence to erase intimations of defeat; Mrs. Leota M. Kellett, director of the Brown County Historical Society, who kindly made available to me the files of the society; and one of New Ulm's most beloved citizens, August Hummel, senior member of the Turnverein, who gave freely of his time and advised me on many points of Turner and New Ulm history. Miss Louise P. Olsen labored excellently in editing and typing the manuscript. Mr. Joseph Shechtman and Miss Marcia Strout, who saw the book through various stages of publication, worked tirelessly to improve it in many ways. My wife corrected the manuscript and gave her skillful assistance in preparing the index. And last, but by no means least, the officers and members of the Turnverein and the non-Turner respondents are the characters in this story; their patience and generosity made it possible. For all errors of fact and interpretation I alone am responsible.

NOEL IVERSON

TABLE OF CONTENTS

I
Theory and Method

¶ chapter 1

GERMANIA AS AN ETHNIC COMMUNITY

IMMIGRANTS, millions upon millions, have been America's most vital import, the bone and flesh and spirit of the American heritage. They set the style and tempo of American life. Each wave of immigrants led to the formation of ethnic communities on American soil. These communities were, so to speak, held briefly in crystalline suspension until the processes of acculturation and assimilation dissolved them in the solution of American society (though they have by no means vanished without a trace). They remained in suspension as long as the national or majority community reacted to their presence with a combination of prejudice and tolerance. America in some measure continues in a fluid state in which at any time the introduction of new aliens may once again precipitate majority–minority reactions which give rise to an ethnic community – such as the postwar immigration of Puerto Ricans to New York City.

This book examines the experiences of one group of German immigrants who, in the mid-nineteenth century, founded a trading and agricultural center in south central Minnesota, at the edge of the frontier. Germania[1] was selected for study because it offers an unusual departure from the normal pattern of the assimilation of an ethnic community to American culture.

Ordinarily, immigrants of relatively low social standing sought

[1] "Germania," needless to say, is a fictitious name. Unless otherwise indicated, names of various clubs, organizations, and individuals have also been altered (in Part III) to preserve anonymity.

3

to improve their lot; the people of the present study, however, German Turners, modified this procedure. Refugees from the revolution of 1848 in Germany, they settled in Germania among workmen and farmers of comparatively inferior class and status. In short order the Turners, seeking to retain their advantage, emerged as an upper status group in their newly founded German town.

A full explanation of the forces that culminated in the present Turner status group in Germania requires a certain historical as well as theoretical perspective. Germania today, as we shall see, is the product of a unique combination of circumstances, but it is no contradiction to say that Germania also brilliantly exemplifies the success story of American settlement and growth.

The Historical Perspective

Events in Europe and in North America set the stage for the appearance of a number of well-to-do German communities in the New World during a few years before the American Civil War. In nineteenth-century Germany the middle classes had at last begun to claim their birthright as a central stratum in the German nation, but they were faced with remnants of medieval institutions which blocked their full participation in the national community long after such obstacles had been removed from the path of the middle classes in England and France. The German Turners (some of whom later founded Germania), patriotic spokesmen for the burgeoning middle classes, were in the vexing position of being at the same time members of a powerless class and of a powerful, rising nation. Feeling that their destiny was being unfulfilled because of an obdurate ruling class, this German middle class rose in revolutionary protest against the governing aristocracy in 1830 and, more violently, in 1848. When their radical aspirations were frustrated, they responded with more than the usual readiness to emigrate to the New World.

Meanwhile, in the New World the vast expansion into the wilderness had created a vacuum in the American middle classes; this same westward movement, the child of optimism nourished by an enormously rich frontier, had already borne a host of utopian experiments. The more adventuresome settlers of the Atlantic seaboard were eager to found businesses and industries in the territories opening in the West. Those who stayed behind formed a stratum of laborers in the New England factories, where they endured in the congested cities "new misery and new hard masters." Particularly in the Midwest, a shortage of skilled farmers and artisans developed; toward the Midwest numbers of the disillusioned political idealists of 1848 were drawn.

They were imbued with a minority psychology which in France and England during the same period was an inappropriate outlook, not found among the well-to-do middle class elements who were already defending their gains in property and position with the same determination as the upper classes. The minority psychology made the migrant Germans ripe for utopian experiments — for the formation of withdrawn communities which could serve to bring to reality their dreams of the good life. And so some came close to repeating the experience of those pioneer utopians in America — Charles Fourier, Robert Owen, Albert Brisbane, Josiah Warren, Henry Edger, Étienne Cabet, and John Humphrey Noyes — who had inspired ideal societies intended once and for all to rid their members of the evils of private property.

But the immigrant Germans of the 1850's were spared the inglorious failures of these unflaggingly romantic early American socialists. For if these Germans hoped for a life free of political and religious oppression, by and large they were not inclined to construct models of ideal societies that bore no relation to reality. Furthermore, they did not possess the frontiersman's disposition to break all ties with traditional society and culture; rather, they shared the colonist's desire to preserve the Old World heritage.[2] They dreamed, not of founding a new community in the wilderness wrested from savages and wild beasts, but of working up a settled community more akin to the long-established peasant villages and small towns of nineteenth-century Germany. The migrant Germans therefore chose to settle on improved land rather than on the virgin

[2] Robert E. Park and Herbert A. Miller, *Old World Traits Transplanted* (New York: Harper, 1921), drew this distinction between frontiersmen and colonists.

land of the frontier. Moreover, whenever possible they chose places with climate and vegetation similar to those in the areas they had come from — just as thousands of colonial Germans, for example, had been drawn to the richly wooded land of Pennsylvania. The generation of Germans who had opposed the Metternich system (or had felt the economic dislocations of that period), and fled their homeland, sought to realize in the New World their frustrated Old World ambitions.

One semiutopian experiment of the migrant Germans of this generation was Germania, U.S.A.[3] First occupying land only recently delivered from the wilderness by a group of German artisans and workmen from Chicago, the settlement would, in all probability, have failed had it not been that, less than three years later, a small party of Turners arrived by way of Cincinnati. Acting on behalf of the Turnerbund, they sought a place where they might establish, free from outside interference, a socialistic community. After a series of misadventures, during which several sites were explored and rejected, they happened upon the present site of Germania. Impressed by the natural beauty of the area, its excellent soil and abundant water, and its heavy forestation, encouraged by the presence of countrymen with similar ideals, the Turners chose this place for their model town. Their utopian venture was soon augmented by the arrival of new settlers from the Cincinnati Turner Society. From less than a hundred and fifty inhabitants a century or so ago, Germania grew to a population of over thirteen thousand in 1965.

The Turners of Germania underwent a dramatic social transformation in the space of a few years, changing from talented ethnic leaders to an Americanized status elite. They founded a community of aliens and hence themselves inclined toward ethnic form; but they were well-to-do middle-class and upper middle-class people which disposed them toward organizing as a status community. Though the background of the Germania Turners created these contrary tendencies, history alone provides no general explanation of the processes of change from ethnic to status community, or in-

[3] See Chapter 3, pp. 53–67, for a more complete discussion of the founding of Germania.

deed of the principles of community formation itself. Herein lies the special task of sociological analysis.

The Theoretical Perspective

The sociologist shares the historian's interest in the formation and disintegration of communities, an unending process with the appearance of randomness and futility. Sociology emphasizes that human relations tend to stabilize, through the formation of habits, and to systematize into communities — structures that aid the survival of individuals. Though it is obvious that human communities are formed for common survival and develop common goals and values, an infinite variety of styles and meanings of life may theoretically emerge from such formations. And though some communities are more deliberately conceived than others, none has ever succeeded in foreseeing all the consequences of its creation, and none has been free of the onslaught of unforeseen events.

The two notable types of community of special interest here, ethnic and status subcommunities,[4] emerge only within the cultural, social, and territorial dimensions of wider communities. Since they exist as subforms of dominant societies, ethnic communities, and to a lesser extent status communities, are particularly subject to the vicissitudes of change in the wider milieu, however well-conceived and carefully launched they may be. Usually they are neither. And though each has similar purposes — group survival amidst an alien majority or the preservation of a special way of life, for example — the structure and position of each kind of subcommunity with respect to the majority society are quite different. The peculiarities of subcommunity life are to be understood on the basis of the general theory of community underlying this study (pp. 9–10).

That theory subordinates territoriality to what is sometimes called "social space."[5] By this is meant the common ground, consisting of social relations and cultural patterns, that transforms a plurality of

[4] Since these are by definition subcommunity forms, this terminology is redundant. To simplify the language, the term subcommunity, which is generic to both ethnic and status variants, will not ordinarily be used in conjunction with "ethnic" or "status."

[5] R. M. MacIver, *Society* (New York: Rinehart, 1937), pp. 150–152; 8–10. MacIver called it "community sentiment" when speaking of its emotive aspect,

people into a community. Territory alone does not provide this common ground, as most sociologists today recognize.[6] Formerly, the idea of community as a system of institutions occupying a territory — introduced into sociological theory by an English student of jurisprudence, Henry Sumner Maine,[7] and incorporated by Ferdinand Tönnies in his famous *Gemeinschaft–Gesellschaft* dichotomy[8] — emphasized territoriality as fundamental to community. Since the 1920's, however, American sociologists' attention has shifted from the ecological and geographic to the social and cultural aspects of communities, as the "social ecology" of Robert E. Park, Ernest W. Burgess, and Roderick D. McKenzie[9] gave way to a broader conception, initiated by R. M. MacIver and by Eduard C. Lindeman,[10] in which community is seen as a system of common life which need not be restricted to a fixed geographical area[11] (although the territorial community — e.g., the band, tribe, or village — is included as a subtype).[12]

"social coherence" when stressing the shared purposes of a group occupying a territory and pursuing a way of life somewhat apart from and yet physically within a larger society.

[6] Hannah Arendt, *Eichmann in Jerusalem: A Report on the Banality of Evil* (New York: Viking Press, 1963), p. 241. An understanding by no means limited to social scientists, as Hannah Arendt, in thinking about the European Jews' legal relation to the state of Israel, says: " 'Territoriality,' as the law understands it, is a political and legal concept, and not merely a geographical term. It relates not so much, and not primarily, to a piece of land as to the space between individuals in a group whose members are bound to, and at the same time separated and protected from, each other by all kinds of relationships, based on a common language, religion, a common history, customs and laws."

[7] Henry Sumner Maine, *Ancient Law* (New York: Henry Holt, 1906).

[8] *Community and Society*, trans. by Charles P. Loomis (East Lansing: Michigan State University Press, 1957).

[9] *The City* (Chicago: University of Chicago Press, 1925).

[10] MacIver, *Community* (New York: Macmillan, 1917), pp. 22–24; Lindeman, "Community," *Encyclopedia of the Social Sciences* (New York: Macmillan, 1934).

[11] One can go too far in this direction also: I do not mean that since MacIver and others conceived this newer idea of community, territory is of little or no importance in the study of human communities, which typically transcend mere physical boundaries. They do, but, again typically, they observe them — at times with awesome ferocity.

[12] This discussion follows Don Martindale's *American Social Structure* (New York: Appleton-Century-Crofts, 1960), pp. 132–133, 147–149, and is informed by John Sirjamaki's *Sociology of Cities* (New York: Random House, 1964), pp. 7–18.

A General Theory of Community Formation

Communities represent, in addition, human groupings which provide for the basic needs of their members. Communities are total ways of life, forming systems composed of sufficient groups and institutions to enable their members to survive the trials of a normal year and a normal life.[13] Sustaining complete cultures as well as total social systems, communities solve the basic problems of human existence: physical subsistence, the socialization of members, the control of individuals and groups, and defense against outside intervention.[14]

These basic imperatives are met differently by each community, for none evolves precisely the same arrangement of institutions or invests them with quite the same meanings and purposes as any other community. Institutions, and the peculiarities of their reciprocal adjustments, contribute to the uniqueness of each community. In the long run, the "interadjustment of the institutions of one area of social life to influences arising out of another"[15] usually leads to the establishment of a distinct way of life, a process which is illuminated by the general principles of community formation underlying this study: *stabilization, consistency,* and *completeness.*[16]

All communities, whether subforms such as ethnic and status communities or the most extensive forms, such as nation states,[17] institutionalize behavior and seek to make citizens' activities stable, consistent, and complete. All communities require, as a condition

[13] Don Martindale, *Social Life and Cultural Change* (New York: Van Nostrand, 1962), p. 44. By "normal" is meant that range of behavior and experience defined as such by a community. See also MacIver, *Society*, p. 9: "The mark of a community is that one's life *may* be lived wholly within it, that all one's social relationships *may* be found within it."

[14] Martindale, *American Society* (New York: Van Nostrand, 1960), pp. 254ff.; and *Social Life and Cultural Change*, pp. 39–44. For an earlier and somewhat more involved discussion of the social and cultural implications of these universal human imperatives, see Bronislaw Malinowski's *A Scientific Theory of Culture* (University of North Carolina Press, 1944), pp. 125–131.

[15] Martindale, *Social Life and Cultural Change*, p. 44.

[16] Martindale, *American Social Structure*, pp. 131–132.

[17] *Ibid.*, p. 133; Sirjamaki, *op. cit.*, pp. 15–18. Nation states are, of course, societies — national communities. The formal distinction between community and society made here is that a society is man's most extensive system of common life and may contain a number of communities, whereas a community represents the most compact ordering of diverse ways of life in societies.

of their existence, that standardized solutions to problems of communal life[18] — institutions — be invented, and that these solutions (which are invested with norms and rules) be made stable. The stabilizing power of institutions is a potent force for community survival. (Tradition marks the organic stability of communities; totalitarianism is the death warrant of tradition.) When, on the other hand, there is but an assemblage of persons, each going his own way, there is no stability in whatever joint efforts may be undertaken and hence no community.

Consistency or pattern must be hit upon if communities are to persist. Behavior and values need to be brought into some general accord (whether formally declared or tacitly understood, the effect — agreement and integration — is the same) if a ruinous competition of redundant institutions is to be avoided.

Finally, the survival of the human community rests upon its ability to provide a total way of life. It is no accident, for example, that societies tend universally to regard chronic bachelorhood as an errant condition, for no society is complete which does not institutionalize (and succeed in upholding) marriage. When a community fails to meet the basic need for institutional completeness sufficient to provide the basic imperatives its existence is imperiled.[19]

Ethnic and Status Communities

I have suggested that human beings exhibit a universal tendency to guide their activities toward community form, that is, to fashion modes of behavior which are stable, consistent, and complete. As a general principle, this tendency operates in all communities — tribes, peasant villages, cities, ethnic communities, or status communities. Ethnic and status communities are special cases of pluralities of aliens or status equals forming inconsonant ways of life within a wider milieu. To account for these particular community types — and thus explain the transformation from ethnic to status community

---

[18] Martindale, *American Social Structure*, p. 306.

[19] This is an uncommon occurrence, for man cherishes the communities he forms; they are the source of his comfort, show the dimensions of his hope. He does not carelessly allow rifts between his institutions to grow so deep that his community's existence is threatened. If possible, the necessary adjustments are made long before that threat arises.

of Germania's Turners — we need to examine the two forms' quite different relations to the majority society and, accordingly, their fundamental social and psychological differences.

The members of every community attempt to monopolize the values created as they worked out a way of life, and to come to the defense of these values whenever forces from outside their community threaten their existence or the distinctiveness of their way of life. The Southern regional community, for example, is currently experiencing the most devastating attack on its cherished beliefs and practices since Emancipation. Under special circumstances, and depending upon its source, this impulse to close against outsiders can contribute to the formation of an ethnic or a status community; but it does not inevitably produce such a community.

Such communities appear, rather, as a result of a combination of forces. The ethnic community is largely the product of contradictory forces of acceptance and rejection which originate in the majority society and are directed toward immigrants. The status community, by contrast, emerges when status equals, capitalizing upon the internal differentiation of their society, close their ranks against outsiders of inferior or superior status.

Though both forms are minority communities existing in complexly structured societies, there is much more of the element of enforced withdrawal in the formation of an ethnic community, which usually happens in response to pressures from the majority (e.g., prejudice or discrimination), than there is in the formation of a status community, which typically appears as a result of internal demands (e.g., snobbery and privilege) to restrict the entrance of aspirants to one's society of status equals.[20]

[20] These processes have been described (Martindale, *American Social Structure*, pp. 377ff.) by means of "secondary" principles: "extra-community closure," which means that ethnic aliens are required by majority hostility to find their own defense and succor their own minority needs; "inner-community closure," in which status-seeking natives protect their own style of life from status-threatening outsiders; "extra-community innovation," which means that the majority society seeks the services and products of its ethnic minorities and thus tolerates their presence; and "inner-community differentiation," in which social differentiation within a society leads to a hierarchical structure (of unequal access to power, wealth, and esteem) and hence to the opportunity for some members of society to monopolize access to these values.

If American society, for example, resists the introduction of aliens, forcing them to develop their own ethnic communities on American soil, and yet allows American natives to create status communities almost at will, American society also encourages ethnic communities and has structural conditions which make creating status communities eminently attractive.[21]

The Ethnic Community. Thus, the wider society reacts to immigrants in its midst — who bring foreign habits, speech, and ideas — in a predictable manner: seeking to protect its monopoly of interests and its total way of life from encroachment and subversion by foreigners, it keeps the aliens semi-isolated, at least socially and psychologically. Specifically, members of certain minority communities are denied a full range of employment opportunities, are kept from settling in some areas, are kept out of native clubs with hallowed traditions. In short, the ethnic community, as a minority or guest element in American society, has been partly closed off from the life of the host community.[22] Full participation in the wider community has been systematically denied the aliens.

Once formed, however, the ethnic community itself tends toward closure, an inner community drive that is reinforced by the prejudice of the majority.[23] Though this development need not be taken up

[21] Theoretically, this statement does not apply in a "classless" society such as the Soviet Union. It finds historical support in the deliberate practice of European monarchs and states of granting special privileges to Jews (at first, mainly to court Jews, international financiers, and other well-to-do individuals; later, to "the whole of Western and Central European Jewry") and of legislating against the assimilation of the Jewish communities into European culture and society (often with the encouragement and sometimes at the insistence of wealthy Jews, whose positions were realistically threatened by the national egalitarian and emancipation movements of nineteenth-century Europe). See Hannah Arendt, *The Origins of Totalitarianism*, 2nd ed. (New York: World, 1958), pp. 11–18.

[22] Martindale, *American Social Structure*, pp. 427ff., 397–398. While not identical with a minority, the ethnic community ordinarily comprises members of a minority. It differs, however, from a minority in its solution to a problem shared by both, namely, the lack of privilege and power in the majority society. The ethnic community is an organized solution to this problem, whereas a minority (e.g., the Negro or the Roman Catholic or the Mexican minority) does not typically form a community. The term *ethnic community* is generic for the guest community in North America.

[23] Thus, for example, the ethnic community places its own restrictions on membership, maintains semisecret associations, and organizes its own social, religious, economic, and (in the case of the Jewish ethnic community) educa-

here, it raises the further question as to how the ethnic community can form in the teeth of resistance from the wider community. If this resistance were complete, the ethnic community could not form. Some tolerance of aliens, therefore, is necessary for the emergence of a minority community. The partial reception of the outsiders into the majority community by reason of their possession of valued talents and knowledge is a universal process.[24]

The special circumstances favorable to the establishment of an ethnic community are created when there is both tolerance of and prejudice against pluralities of aliens rather than single individuals. Pluralities of aliens are needed to form an ethnic community within the wider community. This means that the wider community tolerates or perhaps even invites and welcomes numbers of aliens within its ranks. If, however, the wider community shows complete receptivity toward the aliens, there is little incentive for the alien groups to form a withdrawn community within the framework of the whole. A combination of resistance and reception from the wider community is thus requisite for the emergence of the ethnic community.

Though Germania was formed as an ethnic community in response to the forces just described, a full perspective on it requires an understanding of the status community as well.

The Status Community. Though in many superficial respects the ethnic and status communities resemble one another, a fact which has led some eminent American sociologists (namely, Warner and his associates) to confuse the two, they have very different origins. Ordinarily, ethnic communities first form at the bottom of society, whereas status communities tend to form at the top. The latter may,

tional institutions. Prevented from full access to the values of the majority, the ethnic minority turns to its own traditions, characteristically arriving at a new point of synthesis in what was its peripheral institution (often the church) and has become its core institution. Assimilation is seen by the founders of the ethnic community as undesirable, for it means the gradual revision and then final elimination of their traditional values.

[24] Martindale, *American Social Structure*, pp. 381–384. These contradictory tendencies — resistance and receptivity to aliens — in the society at large are resolved by the establishment of institutions intended to serve both the wish to keep the society intact and the desire to seek the values offered by the outsiders. Historically, the latter may be illustrated by silent trade, family clientage, variations on the theme of diplomacy, fictitious adoption, and naturalization.

it is true, form at the bottom of society — "Hobohemia," for example, was a low-placed status community in American society before the Great Depression.[25] The new middle-class status communities of Park Forest, Illinois, and Drexelbrook, Pennsylvania, further demonstrate that status communities may form at any level of society.[26] American society is interlaced with status communities of great variety, each formed to consolidate and maintain access to general values — for example, the metropolitan Four Hundred or the old Boston elite described by Cleveland Amory.[27]

The differentiation of relations into a hierarchical structure and the closing off of entrance to levels of this structure make possible the formation of the status community; this takes place within the single community.[28] Underlying this process is the shift in the institutional synthesis of the status community. The precise nature of this resynthesis, however, is not the same for both ethnic and status communities. The members of the ethnic community experience the transformation of the peripheral institutions of their homeland into core institutions in the New World, whereas the status community styles itself after institutions of the total society.[29]

A Summary of Contrasts

When the wider community allows a group of foreigners to pursue their own way of life in its midst and yet denies them full access

[25] It was brilliantly explored by Nels Anderson, *The Hobo* (Chicago: University of Chicago Press, 1923).

[26] For an incisive account of the "packaged suburbs" as status communities, see William H. Whyte, *The Organization Man* (New York: Simon and Schuster, 1956).

[27] *The Proper Bostonians* (New York: E. P. Dutton, 1947). For further discussion of status communities in the United States see E. Digby Baltzell, *Philadelphia Gentlemen* (Glencoe: Free Press, 1958) and C. Wright Mills, *The Power Elite* (New York: Oxford University Press, 1956).

[28] Martindale, *American Social Structure*, p. 493.

[29] It is even possible to create a status community which rests primarily upon the systematic rejection of a society's major institutions — the Beats are a notable recent example (in rootlessness and mobility they compare somewhat to the world's coteries of wealthy international pleasure seekers). Here status is reflected in a style of life which holds up an inverted image to conventional society. The precariousness of this type of status community is dramatized when its real or studied nihilism begins to appeal to a mass audience; most of its members soon disperse under the glare of publicity. One is tempted to conclude that nothing destroys like success.

to its opportunities, the immigrants will respond by partial adjustment and partial withdrawal, forming an ethnic community.

The status community forms, on the other hand, when a group of natives develops a sense of honor and a style of life which sets them apart from the majority. It characteristically forms at the upper levels of society, as a monopolistic joining of elitist individuals whose common aim is to consolidate their access to values of prestige, influence, and wealth. It cultivates snobbery and is regarded by outsiders with mixed feelings of resentment and admiration.

It may now be seen why it was necessary to sketch the theory of the status community in order to account for Germania. The theory of the ethnic community supplies the added explanatory power which makes it possible to answer two basic questions: Why did Germania form into an ethnic community rather than into a status community, as one would superficially expect? What processes emerged as a product of the natural operation of forces which made status community structure congenial to Germania's founders?

The Uniqueness of Germania

Germania's uniqueness provoked these questions. The presence of aliens from the outside is not in itself sufficient to account for the formation of an ethnic community, even though they may come in great numbers. Large migrations of English and Scotch to the United States occurred without the forming of English and Scotch ethnic communities. Moreover, non-English immigrants did not necessarily form ethnic communities, as revealed by the attitudes of French Huguenots and of educated Italians who fled from political revolutions. One could perhaps formulate a general principle about the failure of an ethnic community to form in such cases: Whenever the ethnic alien is of as high or higher class and status derivation as the group within which he is moving, he tends to form status communities rather than ethnic communities.

The uniqueness of Germania can be approached from this standpoint: although its German founders were of a higher class and status than the community they settled in, they nevertheless formed into a true if ephemeral ethnic community, thereby reversing the common pattern of ethnic community formation. No ethnic community so formed, however, can long remain a withdrawn community when the values of the surrounding world are open and accessible to its members. The Turners of Germania very soon realized that greater advantages lay in forming an upper status community which would allow them both to monopolize access to the values of the majority and to preserve their distinctive way of life, than in remaining a withdrawn ethnic community. In the transition from an ethnic to a status community, however, the traditions of the founders of Germania would necessarily be weakened.

Hypotheses and Method

Our theoretical and historical understanding of the evolution of the Turners of Germania, from their inception as an ethnic community to their present declining position as an upper status community, may be expressed in the form of two general hypotheses that will guide this study. I. The Germania Turners' marketable talents gave them partial acceptance in America; but in spite of these assets their historical marginality and foreign culture at first forced them into the form of an ethnic community. II. Their superior social and cultural experience, however, when applied to frontier conditions, enabled them to get control of the key positions of influence, prestige, and wealth in Germania. They consequently emerged in their new form as a status elite.

Although in a class and status sense the emigrés who founded Germania were superior to their surroundings, they had cultural and historical peculiarities which provided them an unusually strong inclination to form an ethnic community. For example, as a minority in Germany they had developed a minority psychology. They carried this attitude with them to North America, where they were received with prejudice and hostility. Moreover, they were Germans and aliens, subject therefore to widespread nativist resentment, focused partly in the Know-Nothing movement of the mid-nineteenth century.[30] Many of them were Roman Catholics, a minority religion

[30] At this stage in the history of German-Americans, there was considerable anti-German sentiment, which later declined, only to revive during and after World War I.

under attack by the native Americans, who did not always distinguish between Catholic and non-Catholic Germans. And since the Turners spoke German, they felt a temporary practical advantage in associating with other German-speaking immigrants.

The inducements to form an ethnic community were not all negative, however. The Turners shared in the utopian idealism that was prevalent in North America at the time they arrived. Both their own receptivity to utopian experiment and the tolerance by the surrounding community of such ventures contributed to the formation of an idealistic ethnic community. Their sociopolitical institution, the Turnverein, also served as a new point of orientation of their life in the United States, around which they could readily organize a life of their own. Once they had established their own community, the additional motive to preserve their cultural heritage could be felt. Finally, the United States needed skilled artisans and experienced farmers — stable, industrious people to build new communities at the edge of the expanding frontier. The German immigrants from the 1830's to the 1850's were ideally suited to meet this need.

Thus powerful inclinations, positive and negative, were at work in the Turners' withdrawal to ethnic community life. But for the Germania Turners, the very act of ethnic closure raises a question: can an ethnic community endure when formed of people who have superior class and status characteristics? My second major hypothesis suggests that the answer is no, and tells why not.

It was to the advantage of the Turners, as the founding elite, to invite anybody of low status into Germania. Only by becoming a status community could they full exploit their original superior social and cultural position in Germania. If, on the other hand, the Turners had remained an exclusive German ethnic community, some of them would eventually have had to take menial jobs; as members of an ethnic community, not all could enjoy equally the privileges of high status. By letting in people of lower status, and by forming themselves into a status community, the Turners were able to control Germania's prestigeful and powerful positions.

It can thus be seen that three kinds of immense advantages

accrued to the Turners in forming a status community: *economically* the Turners were in a position to assume most of the top positions and the highest paying jobs; in *status*, the Turners benefited by forming a homogeneous, well-known group which gave them high prestige (in addition, the Turnverein represented an unusually high level of intellectual and cultural interests which, if anything, enhanced the pretensions of its members to status); with respect to *power*, the Turners were able to monopolize access to the limited political positions of the community. None of these advantages would have been possible to an ethnic community.

The Design of the Study

The two-part design of the study, historical and statistical, stems directly from its two broad hypotheses, and represents quite different ways of answering the questions: What historical forces catapulted the Turners into an ethnic community? What structural forces recast them into a status group?

Actions and events external and internal to the Turner community of Germania set these forces in motion. By a comparative evaluation of the German and American milieus, the complex of forces which precipitated the Turner ethnic community will be clarified; by a structural-generational analysis of Germania today the transformation of the style of life and social position of the Turners will be worked out.[31]

In the first part of the study the historical background of the Turners will be reconstructed in enough detail to show how their experience as a political minority in the Old World and as an ethnic minority in the United States led them to found a withdrawn ethnic community, Germania, rather than a status community oriented to the surrounding society.

It is reasonable to expect, however, that when a group like the Turners, consisting largely of middle- and upper middle-class artisans, tradesmen, and professionals, sheds its ethnic orientation and takes on the role of an upper status elite within the community it founded, a series of important changes in its social standing and

[31] See Part II, Chapters 2–3, and Part III, Chapters 4–6, respectively.

18

style of life will take place. The proof of the transformation of the Turners from an ethnic to a status community rests upon two kinds of comparisons, first between Turners and the non-Turner majority (establishing the distinctiveness of the former) and second between first- and second-generation Turners and non-Turners (revealing the main drift in the life and standing of the Turners with respect to Germania).

Employing Mannheim's concept of "generation unit" differentiated on the basis of the "common destiny" [32] members of each unit share, two generations each of Turners and Non-Turners were selected, the former by membership in the Germania Turnverein, [33] the latter randomly from the city directory.

Since the European-born Turners founded Germania, their descendants are the first native-born generation, and will be described in the following account as *Founders*[T]. Their descendants, in turn, are members of the Germania Turnverein. The second-generation native-born Turners may thus be described as *Members*[T]. The original non-Turners came as settlers around the ethnic community;

[32] Karl Mannheim, "The Problem of Generations," in *Essays on the Sociology of Knowledge*, Paul Kecskemeti, trans. (London: Routledge and Kegan Paul, 1952), pp. 303–304. The concept of generations has sociological significance not simply with regard to age but also with regard to the shared meanings and values of people of the same historical and social structural location. The separation in this book of the two generations at age forty-five has meaning, because the experience of members of each generation is different: first-generation Turners and non-Turners reached maturity sometime between the two World Wars and saw their own families through the Great Depression. Their children, forming the populations for our second-generation subsamples, have shared a usually quite different experience. Most of them were too young to feel the trials of the depression deeply; they had no experience of pre-depression times, and they reached maturity in the 1940's and 1950's. Born just before and during the Second World War, they live in a world differing dramatically from their parents'. They form Mannheim's "generation unit," loosely classifiable by common experiences that set them apart, in their values and goals, from the first generation.

The depression was a turning point in the social experiences of the two generations. Changes occurring within the Turners and non-Turners can therefore be expected to be revealed most sharply by a comparison of these first and second generations.

[33] The sample was selected during the summer of 1962 from the membership list (numbering 121) of that year. Since the Turnverein is predominantly a men's organization, only the male members were included in the sample. See Appendix 2 for a detailed discussion of the sampling procedures.

their sons and daughters will be described as *Settlers*[N-T]. Today native-born second-generation non-Turners are not members of Germania's Turnverein, justifying the name *Non-Member*[N-T].[34]

Sample and generational comparisons will be made on four broad dimensions of social differentiation and change: *class, status, power,* and *assimilation.* Each dimension will be explored by means of a scale.[35] The first three scales represent an attempt to quantify the main stratification variables of the study, showing whether Turners are in fact an upper status group who monopolize local values of esteem, influence, and wealth. The assimilation scale tests the expected decline of Turner ethnicity and adoption of American culture. A fundamental part of the questionnaire which was administered to the one hundred and seventy-eight families of the study, the scales were developed from work done by F. Stuart Chapin, W. Lloyd Warner, and August Hollingshead, and were further refined for study of ethnic communities by Alex Simirenko.[36]

[34] Since both Founders and Members are Turners, while both Settlers and Non-Members are non-Turners, all generational subsamples will be marked by the superscripts "T" or "N-T." Thus for all Turners: Founders[T] and Members[T]; for all non-Turners: Settlers[N-T] and Non-Members[N-T]. This will perhaps further clarify the essential Turner versus non-Turner comparison.

Comparisons of these generations required an ex-post-facto design adapted to field conditions. Turners are taken as the "experimental" group (52 Founders[T], 34 Members[T]), non-Turners as the control (55 Settlers[N-T], 37 Non-Members[N-T]). See Appendix, pp. 159–167, for details of the research design and methods of data-gathering and analysis employed in the study.

[35] Perhaps a more accurate, though unwieldy, term would be a "multiple-dimension index," since each scale is in fact a summary indicator of multiple variables whose continuity and homogeneity are not strictly demonstrated. See the Appendix, pp. 162–166, for the rationale of scale construction and the scale items used in this study.

[36] See, for example, F. Stuart Chapin, *The Measurement of Status by the Use of the Social Status Scale* (Minneapolis: University of Minnesota Press, 1933); and revised *Social Participation Scale* (Minneapolis: University of Minnesota Press, 1952); W. Lloyd Warner and Paul S. Lunt, *The Social Life of a Modern Community*, Yankee City Series, Vol. I (New Haven: Yale University Press, 1941); W. Lloyd Warner, Murchia Meeker, and Kenneth Eels, *Social Class in America: A Manual of Procedure for the Measurement of Social Status* (Chicago: Social Research Association, 1949); and for a discussion in the same tradition of the stratification of the ethnic community, W. Lloyd Warner and Leo Srole, *The Social Systems of American Ethnic Groups*, Yankee City Series, Vol. III (New Haven: Yale University Press, 1945); August B. Hollingshead, *Elmtown's Youth: The Impact of Social Classes on Adolescence* (New York: John Wiley, 1949); and August B.

Change in Germania will be analyzed on each scale dimension. In Part II a historical and descriptive analysis of Germania will be made, in which the first general hypothesis is tested. Psychologically and structurally, we shall follow the changing fortunes of the Turners, from their peripheral situation in Germany and North America (which imbued them with a minority outlook), to their central establishment in Germania as a status elite. The manner of derivation of the specific working hypotheses I employed will be reserved for Part III, which embodies the statistical analysis of the scale comparisons.

Recapitulation

Germania, U.S.A., presents an unusual pattern of social and cultural change in the course of the experience of ethnic communities in the United States. Its departure from the normal course is seen in its relative isolation, at the edge of the frontier, from other communities; in the superior class, status, and power situation of its immigrant founders; in their utopian-revolutionary intentions; and, finally, in the transformation of the Germania Turners from a highly placed ethnic minority community to a subcommunity of status elites.

Social change in Germania occurred in two stages: first the founding of the ethnic community, second the shift to status community. Two hypotheses have been set forth to explain these two kinds of change: first, that historical peculiarities gave rise to the ethnic community, and, secondly, that inherent forces led to the re-forming of the original group along status community lines.

Testing these hypotheses requires investigating the historical background of the Germania Turners on the one hand, and analyzing structural changes within the wider community on the other. The second part of that investigation will be based on an instrument designed to gather descriptive data and to provide systematic information about the comparative power, wealth, esteem, and extent

Hollingshead and Frederick C. Redlich, *Social Class and Mental Illness: A Community Study* (New York: John Wiley, 1958); Alex Simirenko, *Pilgrims, Colonists, and Frontiersmen: An Ethnic Community in Transition* (Glencoe, Ill.: Free Press, 1964).

of assimilation of Turners and non-Turners of the first and second generations.[37]

These comparisons, I hope, will reveal something of the dimension and drift of small-town life in mid-twentieth century America. As the crucible of American culture has reduced its diverse immigrant and old elite groups to a common mold, a common experience, a common outlook; and as "the American" becomes a creature everywhere familiar, an entity known by his uniform traits, the experiment in democratic pluralism would seem to have run its course. America's "Little Bohemias" and Nob Hills have succumbed to or joined the drive toward centralism, merging into the standard landscape of mass culture. In this drift of American life lies the larger significance of the Germania experience.

[37] The scales have been demonstrated to be both valid and reliable. See Appendix 2, pp. 166–167.

II

A Historical and Descriptive Analysis

chapter 2

OLD WORLD ROOTS

A FULL appreciation of the uniqueness of Germania as an ethnic community under the Turners requires an understanding of their experience as a minority both in Germany and in North America. Pressures brought to bear on the Turners forced them to become a political minority in Germany, an ethnic minority in the United States. Their experience as a semilegal political action group in Germany imbued them with a utopian fervor and a minority outlook, which in turn impelled them to translate their aspirations into the social reality of an ethnic community in North America.

The dual response of prejudice and receptivity manifest in the host community[1] explains the ease with which the Turners established an ethnic community on American soil. Their thwarted social and political ambitions and their sufferings from religious intoler-

[1] Don Martindale, *American Social Structure*, pp. 427–428. Max Weber, *The Religion of India*, trans. and ed. by Hans H. Gerth and Don Martindale (Glencoe, Ill.: Free Press, 1958), p. 13. The host community is the majority community within which the ethnic, or guest, minority forms. The Turners of Germania were not, however, a guest people in the pure form Weber envisaged: "The purest form of this type is found when the people in question have totally lost their residential anchorage and hence are completely occupied economically in meeting demands of other settled peoples — the gypsies, for instance, or, in another manner, the Jews of the Middle Ages." In the United States the term *ethnic community* is generic for the guest community. An ethnic (or guest) community is one which has lost its original point of synthesis and established a new one in what were its peripheral institutions. The Turners approximated this experience when they founded Germania. For a time they formed an ethnic community of semiminority characteristics, establishing the Turnverein as their transplanted institutional point of integration.

ance in Germany instilled in them feelings of persecution which reinforced their voluntary withdrawal from American culture in the first half of the nineteenth century. A historical reconstruction of the life of the Turners in Germany and in North America will clarify these processes which culminated in the founding of Germania.

The Old World History of the Turnverein

The history of the Turnverein, the primary sociocultural and political institution of the Turners, falls logically into two periods: from 1811, the time of its founding, to 1848 in Germany; and from 1848, the year of exodus, to the present in the United States. The contrasting social and cultural milieus of nineteenth-century Germany and North America set the stage for the Turners' initial political minority status in the Old World and their later ethnic minority situation in the New.

The Origin of the Turnverein. The middle-class bid for power in early nineteenth-century Germany crystallized in the Turner movement when Friedrich Ludwig Jahn established the first Turnplaz on the Hasenheide in Berlin in 1811.[2] The Turnverein was launched as a revolutionary organization composed of powerless bourgeois — petty officials, discontented students, intellectuals and artists, radical journalists, most of them young, all intent on winning a voice in the burgeoning nation.[3] An intense romantic whose temper bore the imprint of eighteenth-century cultural nationalism, Jahn (or "Turnvater Jahn" as he is affectionately known to Turners) sought to overthrow Napoleonic rule and the German aristocracy.[4]

[2] Carl Wittke, *Refugees of Revolution: The German Forty-Eighters in America* (Philadelphia: University of Pennsylvania Press, 1952), p. 147.

[3] Augustus J. Prahl, "The Turner," in *The Forty-Eighters*, A. E. Zucker, ed. (New York: Columbia University Press, 1950), pp. 79–80.

[4] Albert Bernhardt Faust, *The German Element in the United States*, Vol. II (New York: Steuben Society of America, 1927), p. 387. Jahn and his followers cast these aspirations in political-romantic terms, urging physical and mental preparedness for the coming struggle. Jahn's ideal, says Faust, "was to recreate in Prussia the gigantic statures of the ancient Germans, as Tacitus had described them." The main event of later importance to the Turners before the Napoleonic conquest of Germany was the appearance of cultural nationalism, a movement which in the late eighteenth century had begun to alter the social structure of Germany. First appearing as a series of literary and intellectual tendencies, as expressed in the works of Klopstock, Lessing,

In founding the Turnverein and also the national student league (Burschenschaften), Jahn set as his goal nothing less than the establishment of a free and united Germany in which the supremacy of the Volk would be realized.[5] This goal, Jahn believed, would be achieved by a concerted effort of will fused in a regimen of physical exercise on the Greek model and a system of universal patriotic education. Physical culture, the core of the Turner program, was linked to their ultimate goal: "Father Jahn was convinced that there could be no re-birth of Germany unless its people became healthy and strong through a carefully planned program of physical training."[6] Gymnastics was thus a means to this goal — part of the "grand opera conspiracies for national unity" of Jahn and his Turners. They adopted as their motto Juvenal's *mens sana in corpore sano*, and engaged in revolutionary strategies to crush Metternich.

Jahn's attempts to enlist German youth in the cause of national-

Wieland, and later Herder, Schiller, and Shelling, it reflected the growing national aspirations of people throughout Germany.

[5] The contradiction implied in the goal of a "free" nation united by the unconscious force of Volk reveals the romanticist-rationalist duality of the German ethos, which the Turners shared. Jahn and many of his followers were anticosmopolitans, preferring their own organic nationalism, which they regarded as an expression of the peculiar soul of the German people. Cosmopolitan Germans such as Klopstock, Lessing, Herder, Goethe, and Schiller represented an early cultural development (classicism) of the liberal tendencies of rationalists like Carl Schurz, who epitomized the opposite pole in the "two souls" of the German people.

Hannah Arendt (*Totalitarianism*, p. 166) argues, I think correctly, that F. L. Jahn, Ernst Moritz Arndt, and other nationalistic liberals of the time were not racists, even though much of Jahn's writing, for example, was definitely protoracist. Actually, "the organic doctrine of a history for which 'every race is a separate, complete whole' was invented by men who needed ideological definitions of national unity as a substitute for political nationhood." Hans Kohn (*The Mind of Germany* [New York: Scribner, 1960]) presents a similar interpretation.

For further discussion of these elements in German character and thought, see Arthur O. Lovejoy's brilliant exegesis of German Romanticism, *Essays in the History of Ideas* (New York: Putnam, 1960), pp. 183–253; Don Martindale, *Community, Character, and Civilization: Studies in Social Behaviorism* (Glencoe, Ill.: Free Press, 1963), pp. 231–294, for a broad analysis of the psychosocial dimensions of the "two souls" of Germany; and in a series of penetrating insights, the literary and philosophical origins of political collectivism of the right are probed by Peter Viereck, *Meta-Politics: The Roots of the Nazi Mind* (New York: Capricorn Books, 1961).

[6] Wittke, *op. cit.*, p. 147.

ism — "part of a larger program of national re-organization planned and fostered by Baron vom Stein, Alexander and Wilhelm von Humboldt, and numerous of the leading intellects of Germany, such as the poets Ludwig Uhland and Heinrich von Kleist" — met with initial success and ultimate defeat.[7] At first the Turners found support in the Austrian government under Metternich, for the middle class and the ruling class were allied in a common desire to cast off the foreign rule imposed on Germany in 1807, when Napoleon defeated Prussia and Austria at the battle of Jena. At this point in its career, the Turnverein moved into the arena of national politics and was poised on the edge of successful incorporation into dominant institutional structures. Had this happened and had the Turners joined forces with the German government in forming a nation, the development of an outcast Turner minority in Germany, their political misfortune in the Revolution of 1848, their subsequent migration en masse to North America, and the founding of the Turner ethnic community of Germania might never have taken place.

The battle of Jena was of decisive importance in the formation of the German nation, for it changed German nationalism from "aesthetic dilettantism to political dynamite."[8] With the awakening of the German middle class, the idea of a unified Germany (in the late eighteenth century a diffuse and implausible vision) became a program of revolutionary possibility, needing first the defeat of the French to set it in motion, and last the dissipation of aristocratic power to make national unity a hard political reality. For a while the Turners played a vigorous part in awakening the middle classes — stimulating national enthusiasms by their meetings, songs, speeches, poems, and military drill. They adopted the old German black, red, and gold for their flag (used again in 1919 as the flag of the Republic), which Turnvater Jahn explained to his disciples signified "out of the black night of slavery through bloody strife to the golden dawn of freedom."[9]

When the French were routed in the Napoleonic wars, however,

---

[7] Prahl, *op. cit.*, p. 80.
[8] Viereck, *op. cit.*, pp. 57–58.
[9] Prahl, *op. cit.*, p. 85. See also Kohn, *op. cit.*, pp. 81–98.

the position of the Turnverein shifted finally to marginality: it was banned as dangerously radical. In view of the Turners' true intentions and the locus of power in post-Napoleonic Germany, this was not surprising. As long as both the Prussian government and the national revolutionaries faced a common enemy, the French, the basic contradiction between their goals — the prolongation of aristocratic rule as opposed to the creation of a powerful unified German empire — remained in the background. As a middle-class revolt for unity and a redistribution of power, however, the real work of the Turnverein and the student league threatened the aristocracy, who were in no mood to hand over the government to the people. Thus, in 1819, after the defeat of the French, the Prussian government, which had previously abetted Jahn in arousing the indignation of the masses against the French, swiftly reasserted its former authority and suppressed all revolutionary activity. Jahn was arrested as a radical and imprisoned for five years; the gymnastic fields were ordered closed by the king of Prussia; both the Turnverein and the Burschenshaften were banned, as the authoritarian reaction of the then dominant Austrian government culminated in the censorship of the universities and the press under the notorious Karlsbad Decrees of October, 1819.

Systematically quelled by the Metternich system, the Turnverein remained an illegal political reform movement until the interdict was lifted in 1848. The old despotic particularism of German government, reintroduced after the War of Liberation, blunted the edge of the popular nationalistic movement. The Prussian customs union (Zollverein), the work of the Mainz Commission, and the activities of official "curators" at the universities, all marked a wholesale return to aristocratic rule.

The manner in which the Turners responded to governmental repression reflects the split between the rationalist and the romantic poles of nineteenth-century German liberalism.[10] Their bitter reaction to the failure of the German rulers after the Napoleonic Wars

[10] Viereck, *op. cit.*, p. 59. German liberalism in the nineteenth century had two sides, once faced against the Metternich regime and all it embodied, the other turned against the state because it was non-German (international in outlook). The former was liberal-rational, turned to the defense of the indi-

to grant the constitutional government promised the people was expressed in the following verses from two poems written in 1816 and 1817 respectively by one of Germany's earliest political poets, Ludwig Urland:

> Speak first, ye princes here assembled,
> Have you forgot that day of fight,
> When beaten to your knees you trembled
> And bowed before a higher might?
> To save your fame the people rallied,
> They proved them loyal to the core,
> Therefore 'tis yours, who still have dallied,
> To grant them now what once you swore
>
> There is no prince so high in station,
> So high-elect none formed of clay,
> That when for freedom thirsts a nation,
> A royal hand its thirst can stay.
> Is one alone with greedy fingers
> The riches of all rights to grasp,
> While, for a dole, the people linger
> Till slow the royal fist unclasp? [11]

These were the sentiments of the disinherited, the persecuted. Jahn's aim to fuse the German people into an organic unity or Volkstum was blocked by the rise of the Prussian state after 1819.[12] The vidual; the latter was romanticist-revolutionary, favoring "an organic and totalitarian *Volk* state."

The inheritors of nineteenth-century German romanticism, the American Turners a century later held as a general principle that "human society is a living organism, growing and developing steadily in its essence and form." See Ernst A. Weier, *The Work of the Turner Societies* (Indianapolis: American Gymnastic Union, 1919), p. 26.

[11] Prahl, *op. cit.*, p. 81.

[12] Viereck, *op. cit.*, pp. 69–74. Jahn's program of reform required that the German people heed the unconscious forces of folkdom (Volkstum) while breeding for racial purity and speaking a purified German language; that they strive for the unification of all Germany under a central monarchy in which a new nobility of merit rising on the ruins of feudalism would replace the aristocracy and invite the participation of the masses in government; and, to achieve these reforms, the people must promote the supremacy of the "collective good," encourage rule by a strong "savior" in troubled times, establish universal national citizenship and the free ownership of land by all, unify the army and the citizenry, and set up "a common public school education for children of all classes." Hence Jahn was hardly nothing more than a "great advocate of freedom and healthy growth," as Faust (*op. cit.*, p. 387) and more recent writers on the subject have concluded.

Turnverein was forced into a marginal, unstable position in German society; its members were powerless successfully to oppose the ruling groups — princes, Junkers, and Prussian officers. Lacking legitimate means of attaining their goals, they resorted to agitation, petition, and open revolt for the redress of abuses; trapped in a rigid complex of classes, kingdoms, duchies, and principalities, the Turners as well as disfranchised middle class were kept from realizing their ideals on German soil.[13]

The Revolution of 1848: The Exodus

The final attempt by the middle classes of nineteenth-century Germany to wrest power from the aristocracy met disaster in the Revolution of 1848, in which the Turners were centrally involved. "Turner [sic] in large numbers flocked to the black-red-gold banner of the Revolution, fought under Sigel and Hecker in Baden, on the barricades in Dresden, and in the streets of Frankfurt and, when the revolution collapsed, paid a heavy price for their rebellion against the reigning princes."[14] Their shaky position in their society became painfully evident in 1848. Their political fortunes had reached their zenith in 1817, when Turnverein membership increased to 1,074 in Berlin alone and when Jahn received honorary degrees from two major universities; then their fortunes dipped alarmingly in 1819 when Metternich, who understood the significance of Turner gymnastics, warned Prussia: "The gymnastic institution is the real training ground for the university mischief. . . . One has to grasp the evil by the roots"; and they plunged beyond recovery in 1848

[13] *Ibid.*, p. 66. Neither landowners nor peasants, the German Turners were the new middle-class migrants to urban areas whose position in society was uncertain and marginal, for they had little power to challenge the existing order and lacked the prestige of family heritage that would open doors to economic or political opportunity. The recognition that they lacked power led them either to sour grapes criticism of the old aristocracy or sublimated denial of the worth of power, criticism usually taking the form of an excessive preoccupation with artistic and intellectual pleasures on the one hand or a frank denunciation of the refined life on the other. Thus while many Turners celebrated the arts and the intellectual life, others, following the example of Jahn himself, were deliberatly crude, offensive, and unpolished in speech and manner. To Jahn, "virtue meant the tough, straightforward Nordic in contrast with the sly French dandy."

[14] Wittke, *op. cit.*, p. 148.

when the Turner minority failed in its abortive struggle to establish a constitutional government.[15]

Thus the Turners found themselves socially impotent and politically outcast in their own country. Most of them turned to the New World for the realization of their thwarted ambitions; a new hope-filled beginning awaited them in North America, a land that promised what they yearned for — Lebensraum — room to build, to grow, to experiment in, a place free from the restrictions on political intentions and religious practices which they found intolerable in Germany. Their mood in the twilight of the 1848 Revolution, a mood of disenchantment tempered in the quick flame of utopian zeal, is captured in the last stanza of a poem by G. Sulzer written about Hecker, the "hero of the Revolution," which bids the political refugee of the Revolution good fortune:

> Now fare thee well! Our hopes go with thee roaming;
> Fortune attend thee o'er the ocean's swell;
> We shall stand fast, for all the Prussian's foaming —
> Lo! at his feet yawns wide the mouth of hell.
> Take for a pledge this happy expectation,
> Nurse it with joy on far Columbia's strand;
> Soon brothers all, we'll build one German nation,
> Then, O our loved ones, back to thine own land! [16]

The refugees of the Revolution turned their backs on the old order, odious and beyond repair, and cashed in all their hopes on a gamble of far better odds across the sea. The "Immigrant's Song," written by Nikolaus Lenau during the Metternich period of repression of the liberals, expresses the Turners' sentiments at the most critical stage of their career:

> For the last time thy name I greet,
> O fallen so low, my Fatherland,
> Who stoop'st to kiss a despot's feet,
> In dull obedience to command.
>
> .   .   .   .
>
> O thou new world, and Freedom's world,
> Against whose fertile, flowery strand

---

[15] Viereck, *op. cit.*, pp. 81–82; and Viereck, *Conservatism Revisited*, rev. ed. (New York: Collier Books, 1962), p. 73.

[16] Prahl, *op. cit.*, p. 90.

The tyrant's wrath in vain is hurled,
In thee I greet my Fatherland! [17]

On the eve of their departure for the United States the Turners were imbued with a minority outlook and a psychology of resentment. As a peripheral institution formed to unify the German empire, the Turnverein was diametrically opposed to the two most powerful institutions of Germany — Austria and Prussia. As a hyperactive nationalist society in fundamental tension with the dominant powers the Turnverein under Jahn's guidance failed to establish popular education or to abolish class privileges as key strategies in their aim, the creation of a Volk state.

The Turnverein in the New World

The Turners who migrated to the United States in the decade after the Revolution were one of the most active utopian-revolutionary segments of the political refugees known as the Forty-Eighters — all middle-class liberals, radicals, and republicans of wide talents and varied backgrounds who had ventured and lost in the movement to make Germany united.[18] The arrival of the Forty-Eighters, Turner and non-Turner, signaled the emergence of the German-American as a vital element in American culture.[19] The Forty-Eighters were unique in the history of American immigration. They provided an unusual intellectual, political, and cultural leadership in the United States at a time when the German settler, and the immigrant in general, were under attack by nativists. The Forty-Eighters transformed the German-American from an

[17] *Ibid.*, p. 83.
[18] Wittke, *op. cit.*, pp. 147–159; and *We Who Built America* (Buffalo, N.Y.: Western Reserve Press, 1939), pp. 188ff. Using the term Forty-Eighter to designate a type of German immigrant is misleading, for most refugees of the 1848 Revolution came to the United States in the 1850's. Though not all Forty-Eighters took part in the Revolution, as used here the term refers to those who actually had taken part in the liberal movements and the revolutions of 1848–1849, and left Germany mainly for political reasons. (The primary cause of the German immigration of the 1850's was economic.) The Turners, who spearheaded the movement for unity, were more involved, politically, in the events of that year than non-Turner Forty-Eighters.
[19] Wittke, *Refugees*, p. v. Wittke observes that the Forty-Eighters "furnished the vitalizing intellectual transfusion which not only affected their fellow countrymen but influenced materially the political and social history of America during one of its most critical periods."

object of scorn and ridicule to one admired and respected.[20] The early history of the Forty-Eighters and the Turners in North America suggests, however, that they were received with both prejudice and tolerance.[21]

Turnerism did not get under way in the United States until the arrival of the Forty-Eighters. Though prominent Turners — notably Karl Beck, Karl Follen, and Francis Lieber (who later achieved wide recognition as a political scientist and encyclopedist), all of whom gave instruction in German literature or physical education in such renowned places as Harvard and Round Hill Boys' School of Northampton, Massachusetts — had introduced Jahn's system of gymnastics as early as 1824, they were exceptional.[22] The real impetus toward Turnerism was the mass exodus of German refugees (though ten thousand sought asylum in Switzerland) to the United States, many of them intent on realizing Turnverein ideals in their adopted country, others pressing for a second republican uprising in Germany.[23]

Their ideals were lofty, often hopelessly impractical, and infused with revolutionary ardor, winning them the admiration of fellow German-Americans and the hostile contempt of nativists. Though many refugees emphasized the physical fitness principles of the Turner movement, their interest in liberal reforms overshadowed, in the United States as it had in Germany, the purely social or cultural. "The *Turnvereine*, like the *Freie Gemeinde* and *Freimän-*

[20] *Ibid.*, pp. 15, 147. "In general, the German element was not highly regarded before the Civil War, and its own lack of self-respect did not improve the situation. Although the ability of individual Germans was readily recognized, Germans as a class were referred to as 'damned Dutch,' and German farmers, artisans, innkeepers, and small businessmen were considered inferior to the average American."

[21] See pages 10–13 for a discussion of the theoretical significance of the ambiguity of nativist reaction to the German immigrant, which set in motion strong tendencies toward withdrawal into ethnic community form.

[22] Prahl, *op. cit.*, pp. 91–92; Wittke, *Refugees*, p. 148.

[23] Wittke, *Refugees*, pp. 92–108. For example, in the late 1840's and the early 1850's plans for a second German revolution were rife in England and America. Radical Forty-Eighters sought to enlist the aid of the United States in overthrowing Metternich. Reaction against this grew to such proportions in the United States that Hecker advised the Forty-Eighters to abandon their utopian visions, their "sickly yearnings" for revolution, and turn instead to the defense of liberty in the United States.

nervereine, to which many Turner belonged, became centers of German radicalism in the abolitionist movement of the 1850's, and in the Civil War hundreds of their members served in the Union Army."[24]

A New Milieu. It is not only in the ideals of the Turners themselves but also in the characteristics of the North American environment — widely different from the German — that an understanding of their experience in the United States is to be gained.

The moment the Turners arrived on North American shores the need to accommodate themselves to "this rude land, wide and free" was impressed upon them. The dimensions of their adjustment are suggested in the contrasts between nineteenth-century Germany and North America. The Turner, like most German immigrants, met at midcentury a nation engaged in a venture of vast scale and historic consequence: the exploration and conquest of frontiers new and challenging to man's ingenuity and sheer physical endurance, to his compassion, understanding, and courage, a venture that strained the fibers of mind and muscle, and fused the passions of men, an experiment in frontier democracy.

The style of control of man and nature in nineteenth-century North America was strikingly unlike what the Turners had known in the fatherland. Here was a nation where the middle classes took as their natural right what had been ruthlessly denied the Forty-Eighters: a share of the common wealth and a voice in affairs of state (as well as the rare privilege of flouting the national interest with impunity). The immense plains and forest wilderness, abundant water, mineral and animal resources, the ever-shifting loci of power, the presence of diverse peoples seeking their fortunes in the absence of a single dominating influence except the challenge of nature — these elements in the environment cast the main social forces of the nation into a materialistic mold and kept the structure of American society open and flexible, unusually tolerant of foreign elements and private endeavors even when they ran counter to the country's stated interests.[25]

[24] *Ibid.,* p. 148.
[25] For a delightful account of American utopian communities, see Alice Felt Tyler, *Freedom's Ferment* (Minneapolis: University of Minnesota

The Turners who came to the United States found on the one hand the cultivation and idealization of precisely what they had fought for in Germany – social equality and political democracy. The particularism and totalitarian stability of German society was anathema to Americans, for whom "movement became a virtue, stability a rather contemptible attitude of mind"; whereas for the Germans order had long been indispensable to justice, disorder and class mobility suspect.

From the very beginning, American life was competitive from the top downward. There was no real stability, no real security for anyone. Here and there a family might stay put; here and there mere stability paid well enough. But such cases were few, and fewer still the fortunes, the social and political positions, preserved over centuries without repeated effort, without setbacks and windfalls. . . . The would-be gentry unlearned the idle lessons of gentility or sank into poverty or returned to the easier world they had left. From the beginning it was "root, hog, or die."[26]

Nor was this a superficial fact about the formation of American society. "What was lacking in America," observes Parkes, "was any deeply felt sense of a social order to which the individual regarded himself as subordinate and through which he could achieve self-realization."[27] Europeans (in this instance the Germans), believed in organic harmony and the sanctity of social institutions which Americans regarded with scornful incomprehension.

The American Reception. On the other hand, though in many respects American society was receptive to foreigners, for some native Americans the egalitarian spirit did not extend to the German immigrant. The ambivalence of Americans toward refugees

Press, 1944). Nineteenth-century America was full of idealistic experiments in social planing – utopian communities such as Oneida and New Harmony, religious communities like those of the well-known and still thriving Mormons and Quakers, Mennonites and Amish, as well as brief and obscure immigrant communities established as states within the United States to perpetuate Old World customs; all were cultural islands on American soil, all enjoyed surprisingly little opposition from the federal government, few survived beyond the first years of dreamy enthusiasm.

[26] D. W. Brogan, *The American Character* (New York: Alfred A. Knopf, 1950), pp. 6–7.

[27] Henry Bamford Parkes, *The American Experience* (New York: Random House, 1959), p. 193.

from the German Revolution was already apparent in 1848. The initially sympathetic American response to the 1848 Revolution came largely from the German-Americans, who had shown mild concern about the revolutionaries and shared their interest in German unification and reform. For example, in 1844 a German society met at the Astor House in New York to support the cause of the German liberals, adopting their black, red, and gold emblem and toasting "a free and united Germany." The German-American press was delirious in its praise of the revolt: "News of the uprising in the German states swept like wildfire through the German-American group. 'France is free. Revolution in Bavaria,' read the headlines. . . . For several weeks the 'glorious news' proved so exciting that German-language editors lacked words sufficiently strong to express their satisfaction with what was happening in Europe." [28]

German radicals in the United States conspired to abet the Revolution; revolutionary clubs appeared overnight in the larger cities to raise money for arms to fight Prussia: "In passionate oratorical flights, and with tears streaming down their cheeks, spokesmen for the Germans and French of New York sang the 'Marseillaise' and demanded that the Rhine frontier between these historic enemies be abolished." [29] While crowds of thousands attended meetings in triumphant celebration of the uprising (such as the great Revolution-fest in New York in 1848), agents of the German governments reported from the United States the plots of American "demagogues and workers" to establish a German republic, noting the extreme disfavor with which the wealthier German merchant class viewed such a challenge to law and order.

The most fervid support of the Revolution came from liberal Germans, whose attitude was expressed in the resolutions adopted by Germans in the "Latin settlement" [30] of Belleville, Illinois, in

[28] Wittke, *Refugees*, p. 30.

[29] *Ibid.*, p. 38. The Philadelphia *Freie Zeitung* pointed out (1848) that German-American support of the Revolution was more rhetorical and emotional than financial, that "German workers, with little to give, were more generous than the well-to-do, and middle-class German merchants regarded revolutionary changes of any kind with suspicion."

[30] Faust, *op. cit.*, Vol. I, p. 442. "The epithet, 'Latin Farmers,' has commonly been applied to the scholarly German settlers, who became quite nu-

1849: "Years have passed since we bade our native soil the last fond adieu. . . . We do know German affairs, for they have driven us hitherwards. We know what is possible, for we see accomplished here what we wish for you. We are no better than you are, but our laws and institutions are better than yours. . . . Only through liberty comes union such as Germany needs."[31]

American support of the Revolution, at best sporadic and centered in middle-class liberal elements, faded with the failure of the Frankfurt parliament. Though "there was hardly an American community of any size where the German Revolution did not prompt . . . expressions of sympathy and support," American opinion was divided over the value of the Revolution; as the Revolution waned, newspaper comment (expressing in part the attitude of the United States government) became more critical of the failure of the German liberals to achieve concrete results. Roman Catholic opposition mounted, condemning revolution in principle and joining with those who regarded the leaders of the Revolution as irresponsible communists whose intention was to destroy private property.[32]

Finally, even the enthusiasm of the German-language press cooled: it began to debate Germany's readiness for a republic, and to compare in unfavorable terms the Frankfurt parliament with the American Constitutional Convention of 1787, usually ending its editorializing with the comment that "Germany is not America." Indeed, the editor of the Columbus *Wesbote* concluded in disgust over the political naïveté of the Frankfurt group that had Christ himself tried to free the German people, He would have been crucified a second time.[33]

Thus the mood in the United States toward the refugees of the German Revolution was not wholeheartedly uncritical; for several reasons the atmosphere in which the newly arrived Forty-Eighters

merous about the revolutionary periods of 1830 and 1848, a class of cultivated men, yet frequently unpractical, for whom manual labor proved a hard school of experience." Their German gymnasium education in Latin and Greek prompted the wide use of the term "Latin settlement."

[31] Wittke, *Refugees*, pp. 35–36.
[32] *Ibid.*, pp. 34, 38.
[33] *Ibid.*, p. 40.

and Turners[34] found themselves grew more chilly and tense, and then exploded in open antagonism to their presence.

This reaction was partly the psychological manifestation of the social factors leading to the formation of ethnic communities in the United States. These factors — seen from two perspectives, the

Table 1. German Immigration to the United States
in Selected Years, 1821–1854*

Year	No. of Immigrants	Year	No. of Immigrants
1821–1830 ...	6,761	1848	62,684
1832	10,000+	1849	63,148
1834	17,000	1852	152,106
1837	24,000	1853	150,094
1847	82,473	1854	229,562

*Wittke, *Refugees*, pp. 12, 43; see also Wittke, *We Who Built America*, pp. 187–188, and Faust, *op. cit.*, Vol. I, pp. 582, 585–586; Vol. II, pp. 24, 27. Faust is the source of the 1821–1830 estimate. The first crest of the immigrant wave was reached in 1854; after 1855 German immigration began to drop, totaling not quite 150,000 by 1873, though it soared to a record high of 250,630 in 1882. The total German influx from 1845 to 1854 came to slightly over a quarter of a million; German immigration by decades from 1830 to 1890 was close to 20 per cent of the total immigration (by 1900, according to Faust, persons of German blood numbered between eighteen and nineteen millions, or about 27 per cent of the total white population of the United States). More than 5,300,000 Germans entered the country during the century before World War I.

points of view of both native-born Americans and immigrants (in this case, German) — have arisen from the intersection and clash of political, economic, religious, and cultural (in the popular sense) interests. An understanding of the formation of the Turner ethnic community of Germania presupposes a knowledge of the major

[34] Since the Turners were in most respects the most vociferous, revolutionary, and militant element of the Forty-Eighters — they form a microcosm of the German immigrant group which fled the Revolution of 1848 — the following discussion of the nature and history of the Forty-Eighters in America may be considered, unless otherwise shown, to represent an expanded image of the Turners. The discussion takes this form of necessity, because more is known about the Forty-Eighters than about the Turners in the United States.

components of such formation: the immigrant Turner minority and the native American majority.

Nativism. The arrival of thousands upon thousands of Germans (see Table 1) in the United States altered the nature of American response to the alien and extended the dimensions of response beyond the small German-American element, drawing in the native-born American majority as well. The native Americans' growing hostility toward the German immigrants was partly a reaction to the sharp increase in immigration in the 1840's and 1850's. The Germans became more noticeable in sheer numbers. More important, however, was the response of native Americans to the "second-era" German immigrant (1830 and 1848), who differed greatly in outlook and expectation from the "first-era" immigrant (the 1700's to the 1820's).[35]

Before 1848 the German element in the United States, descendants of two main waves of immigrants — the first in colonial times, the second in the 1830's — was made up largely of "simple, rural people of good peasant stock," of whom the Pennsylvania Germans were outstanding. German immigration before 1848 was small; it exceeded 10,000 in 1832, reached 17,000 in 1834, and in 1837 was 24,000. Most immigrants of that period were peasants who quickly adapted themselves to a rural existence in self-sufficient, slightly clannish farming communities.[36] The presence of these first-era Germans had not been considered a threat by native Americans. For one thing, these immigrants' services were in great demand; they were skilled and industrious farmers — the remarkably successful New York and Pennsylvania Germans, for example — and for another, "their participation in American affairs, political or otherwise, was of minor importance."[37]

[35] John A. Hawgood, *The Tragedy of German-America* (London: Putnam, 1940). The terms are Hawgood's; he refers to two distinct periods of German-American culture: the original immigration of German farmers who tended to retire into semi-isolated communities of their own, followed in the nineteenth century by a second class of artisans, laborers, professionals, and intellectuals, whose aspirations were quite different.

[36] Wittke, *Refugees*, pp. 6–12; Martindale, *American Social Structure*, pp. 105–110.

[37] Wittke, *Refugees*, p. 9. The Germans' skill in farming is renowned, their production of implements and furniture is praised by collectors of early

The American environment was also tolerant of the second half of the first-era German immigrants (before 1848), who likewise were seeking work in shops and on farms. The German farmer of this group "helped conquer the Mississippi Valley for agriculture, and German artisans, trained in the rigorous apprentice system of the old world, found a profitable market in America for their mechanical skills." [38] They were well received in the United States because their abilities were much in demand and they preferred to remain uninvolved in the political life of the nation.

Divisions in the Ranks of German-Americans. The arrival of the 1848 Germans transformed the German-American element. The Forty-Eighters were appalled by the pervasive political apathy, intellectual incompetence, and low cultural activity of their fellow countrymen in the United States. Despite attempts by leaders to keep alive the political, cultural, and intellectual interests of the Germans in America, these interests had fallen to a low point by 1850. Their native language was poorly spoken, their culture neglected, their politics a disgrace: the Germans in America were accused of trading their votes for free beer provided by ward heelers on election day. "German observers from abroad bemoaned the fact that their countrymen in the United States were reduced to the same low intellectual level as the Irish." [39] The Germans themselves, divided on basic issues between the liberal, free-thinking element and the orthodox Protestants and Roman Catholics, were not only unable to preserve their customs and language, but were also failing to promote their own system of education or to secure equal status with non-Germans.

Though intellectual and cultural activity among the Germans in the United States did not originate with the Forty-Eighters and Turners, it was powerfully stimulated by them. Culturally and intel-

American art. The "Pennsylvania Dutch," as they came to be known, kept to themselves and prospered by careful husbandry and intensive and diversified farming. They created a distinct way of life, an art and a lore rich and enduring. Their descendants spread westward into all parts of the United States, and northward into Canada. Though gradually they lost contact with the old country, they did not become assimilated into American culture.

[38] *Ibid.*
[39] *Ibid.*, p. 15.

lectually superior to the majority of Germans in North America, the Forty-Eighters and the Turners began upon their arrival to assume leadership over the German-Americans and to promote their ideas with a militancy and zeal that won them the disapprobation of both their German and their non-German neighbors.[40]

The older German-American leadership looked upon the energetic efforts of the Forty-Eighters and the Turners to elevate the social and mental life of their countrymen as a threat to their position. It did not matter that the new element was well equipped to provide such leadership, or that the German groups, already on the defensive before nativist attacks, were in need of it. Though many Turners and Forty-Eighters were "men of character, ability, and spirit who were fitted by education and experience to lead their fellow German immigrants,"[41] they came with more verve than judgment, more passion than wisdom, eager to achieve in North America what had been denied them in Germany.

The would-be reformers were inclined not to compromise their ideals, and were highly critical of the shortcomings of German and non-German Americans. Brash young reformers, their "heads full of hollow theories about liberty," the Forty-Eighters and Turners ridiculed the American habit of going to "human bull fights," of retiring into churches on Sunday (a "day of gloom"), of being com-

---

[40] *Ibid.*, pp. 14, 44. "Actually the arrival of the self confident, impatient, and aggressive reformers of 1848, who wanted to make the world over in a day, produced deep seated antagonisms between the older and the newer leadership." Evidence from German and American sources, Wittke notes, indicates that while the bulk of the German immigrants to America after 1848 came from the farming class — "figures from Baden for the period from 1850 to 1855 indicate that farmers constituted 50.7% of the immigration" — a significant number were artisans (26%) and the remainder were of various categories, from laborers to journalists, teachers, and artists. A high proportion of the Turners were men of considerable education and talent, men who had more familiarity with religious, political, and philosophical issues, for example, than their fellow German-Americans of whatever period. See also Faust, *op. cit.*, Vol. II, pp. 389–391.

[41] Wittke, *Refugees*, p. 58. Their active role in the political and cultural affairs of the United States was a more or less unconscious reaction to their failure in Germany: "Their efforts to breathe a new spirit of liberty into a decaying Germany had lost them home, property, jobs, and social position. In an America without kings and princes, petty bureaucrats, state police, state church, or censorship, they were prepared to try again to make a living and to expound their theories of reform."

pletely preoccupied with "business." They deplored the low level of American politics, the undeveloped state of education, and the widespread lack of appreciation for art, music, and literature.[42]

In their disillusionment with American conditions, in their impatience to see their ideals embraced by the majority, in their untempered optimism and overweening sense of mission, the newcomers precipitated antagonisms with the older generation of Germans which led to a deep rift between the "Grays" and the "Greens." A prolonged struggle broke out among the journalists, the Grays denouncing the Greens as unrealistic young hotheads ignorant of American affairs, the Greens attacking their elders as reactionaries whose leadership was a record of bumbling incompetence.[43] There is little doubt that the Greens were themselves largely responsible for the hostility they met: "Their blunt, impolite manners, their pettiness in debate, and their hypocritical attitude toward most things American and German-American did not help matters. The intellectuals among the Forty-Eighters included many who were both immodest and extremely intolerant of the opinions of others, and they labeled as reactionaries, compromisers, and cowards all those with whom they happened to disagree."[44]

Though considerable bad feeling toward the Forty-Eighters emanated from the old German element in the United States — and the disputes among German-Americans were as fierce as between nativists and foreign born — the most extensive and decisive prejudice toward the Greens, a generalized reaction which for a time threatened to drive the German (and Irish) immigrants into ghetto-like groups, came from the Know-Nothing Party. Militant American nativism put the Forty-Eighters on the defensive and offensive for several decades. Nativism presented a common danger to the Grays and Greens which, in conjunction with their shared sacrifices in the American Civil War, and their joint opposition to Sunday blue

[42] *Ibid.*, pp. 71–75.

[43] *Ibid.*, p. 73. For a general discussion of the radical Forty-Eighters, see also "The Radicals," by Eitel W. Dobert, in Zucker, *op. cit.*, pp. 155–181. Dobert observes that the Greens taunted the Grays for their lack of spirit in the fight against Puritanism and slavery.

[44] Wittke, *Refugees*, p. 60.

laws and other religious practices of the majority, went far to heal the breach between them.

Though nativist reaction against the German immigrants was caused by complex motives, the basic reasons for it are not hard to understand: the natives responded as any people might to the presence of aggressive foreigners. The Germans were aliens who pridefully clung to their foreign ways, introducing strange ideas in a strange tongue; espousing dangerous economic, political, and religious doctrines; conspiring to launch a second revolution in Germany from North American shores; criticizing the cultural life of Americans; organizing companies of militia, anarchist societies, associations of freethinkers, and various leagues to promote drinking on Sunday, cremation, the abolition of slavery, and female emancipation: all abhorrent to many native Americans.

The presence of these bold and articulate foreigners, industrious as well as talented, threatened not only the Grays but also native-born Americans. Though the politics of the United States since colonial times had never been entirely free of nativism, hostility toward the immigrant was unusually fierce in the 1850's (it became hysterical in 1915, the year W. J. Simmons revived the Ku Klux Klan). Native resentment of the foreigner mounted when extraordinarily heavy immigration of Irish and Germans introduced the possibility of a captive foreign vote, when the presence of jobless newcomers was regarded by conservatives as a cause of higher taxes, and when immigrants began to compete for jobs, thus lowering the standard of living for all.

Anti–Roman Catholicism also formed a major rallying point among American Protestants, who feared the growing representation of the Church of Rome, strengthened by the influx of Irish and, less so, of German Catholics. While the Irish received the most attention from the secret Know-Nothing Party (whose power alarmed old-line politicians; some factions seriously feared the election of a Know-Nothing president in 1856), the Germans, and especially the radical Forty-Eighters and Turners, bore a generous measure of its abuse. Anti–Roman Catholic nativists made little distinction between non-Catholic Turners (who were denounced by the Roman Catholics for their agnosticism) and Roman Catholic Germans. Moreover, Roman Catholic Germans as well as non-Germans were pitted against irreligious Turners.[45]

Nativism and the Turners. Forced to organize defenses against nativist attacks, the German element in the United States experienced an awakened sense of cultural distinctiveness which slowed the normal processes of acculturation and intensified ethnic isolation. The more radical among the Germans, feeling an exaggerated sense of their political importance, became hyperactive spokesmen for their beleaguered countrymen. Furnished with the issue of nativism, they emerged as leaders in building "little German cultural islands in the great sea of Americanism."

The Turners, very active in the conflict between Germans and nativists, were in conflict with the latter in several respects. State and federal bodies sought to curb the radicalism of the Turnvereine; on one occasion the New York legislature refused to grant a charter to a Turnverein on the grounds that it might become a "front" for anarchist activities. The *Sachem*, a nativist paper of the same state, launched a series of attacks on the Germans, placing them in an inferior caste position somewhere between the Negro and the native Yankee. The anticlericalism and socialism of the Turners fell under heavy criticism from the American press and pulpit.

Several riots broke out between the nativists and the Turners.[46] In New York rioting between Turners and "rowdies" and "short

[45] *Ibid.*, pp. 122–143. Turner anticlericalism had its roots in the fact that the church in Germany had supported the old regime and helped crush the revolution. The Forty-Eighters were divided into rationalist and romanticist wings, both in revolt against dogmatism (while in some measure espousing a dogmatism of their own); some were deists, others atheists or agnostics. According to Wittke, a good many, including the Turners, ranted against Roman Catholicism and Puritanism in language no less temperate than that of their enemies, who answered with the cries of "beer-fogged skeptics" and "hair-lipped [sic], infidel red Republicans." In the heat of religious controversy, German stood against German; blood was shed in furious encounters in Wisconsin between freethinkers and German Roman Catholics.

[46] *Ibid.*, p. 186. "In the recorded cases of mob violence, the Turner [sic] seem to have been involved more often than any other group. Their agnosticism and radicalism made them special targets for conservative, church-going native Americans, and when they organized military companies in self-defense to police their outdoor celebrations, American nativists became alarmed by this 'armed minority' within the state."

boys" began as early as 1850. Often the Turners themselves, by their defiance, provoked attack, and often rowdies deliberately precipitated clashes with Turners by invading their picnics and outings. In 1854 police broke up a Turnfest in Philadelphia on the charge that it was disturbing the peace. The most violent encounters occurred in 1855 in Cincinnati, Columbus, and Louisville, cities inhabited by numerous well-organized Forty-Eighters and Turners. Cincinnati was plunged into a state of civil war for three days in April of that year, when Turners mobilized their sharpshooters and barricaded themselves against angry mobs to protect the German sector of the city.[47] Shortly thereafter, on the Fourth of July (known as the "Bloody Fourth" in Turner annals of Columbus), a company of Turner Jäger marching home from drill and rifle practice in celebration of American independence, were besieged by rock-throwing nativists, whom they answered with rifle fire, wounding three persons and killing a fourth. Police raided the German sector of Columbus, searching homes without warrants and arresting citizens, while a mob gathered, shouting "kill the damned Dutch," and "hang the damned Hessians."[48]

Though Know-Nothing hostility reached its height in 1855, battles between nativists and foreign born continued until the end of the decade. In 1856 in Covington, Kentucky, the Turners were attacked while dedicating their new flag; two years later in Baltimore the police raided a meeting of Turners in the hall of the Social Democratic Turnverein; the following year saw fresh outbursts in Louisville and Cincinnati. In the Covington engagement two deputies were slightly wounded, and a hundred and six Turners were arrested and released on bail of $1,000 each.[49] Though less violent, similar clashes took place in other large cities.

In response to the general threat, the German-language press "urged its readers to unite into a solid phalanx and vote as a unit against the enemies of the foreign born."[50] The decisive contest

[47] Faust, *op. cit.*, Vol. II, pp. 391–393.
[48] Wittke, *Refugees*, pp. 186–187.
[49] *Ibid.*, p. 188; Prahl, *op. cit.*, p. 95. Prahl recounts that only thirty-one Turners were indicted for felony and released under $2,000 bail each. Wittke's sources, however, are more immediate.
[50] Wittke, *Refugees*, p. 189.

shifted to the battle for the German vote. The Know-Nothings vowed to prevent any foreigner from running for public office; they succeeded several times in driving naturalized citizens from the polls. Germans aligned themselves with the newly formed Republican Party (despite the presence of many Know-Nothings in its ranks), meeting the attack of nativists, Democrats, and Roman Catholics with vituperative language. The campaign for the German vote reached a new low in political oratory when, in 1855, a speaker referred publicly to "the lop-eared, big-mouthed, thick-headed Dutchman . . . the foam of beer still in his horse-tail mustache, and stinking . . . of garlic and onions."[51]

Turners backed Republican standard-bearer Frémont, whom they represented as the candidate of "labor and the settler"; Seward of New York won great favor among the Germans for his consistent opposition to all forms of nativism; liberal Forty-Eighter Carl Schurz toured the nation for the Lincoln ticket during the campaign of 1860, traveling twenty-one thousand miles and causing strong reactions wherever he spoke. German Turners held jubilant torchlight processions in Schurz's honor while the Democratic press attacked him as "a red Republican, save for his heart, which is black." In the Midwest, huge crowds composed largely of Germans greeted "that tremendous Dutchman"; solidly Republican Germania turned in a vote for Lincoln exceeding that for Douglas by five to one.[52]

On all sides — in politics, in religion, in the press, and in the streets — the German element in the United States reacted to nativist attack by closing ranks against both nativists and moderate Germans, labeling all "Anglo-Americans" as nativists and all Germans who refused to enter the combat against the "common foe" as traitors to their own kind. The nativist issue was extinguished by the Civil War, but not before strong tendencies had been generated among many Turners and non-Turners to retire from the strife-filled urban scene to a place at the border of the frontier where they could cultivate a life of their own in peace. One such actual venture of unusual success and longevity became Germania, U.S.A.

[51] *Ibid.*, p. 205. The same statement was attributed to another speaker in the campaign of 1864.
[52] *Ibid.*, pp. 203–218.

Before this story is told, however, its background in the North American Turner movement must be presented. For in all likelihood Germania would never have appeared without the support of the national Turner organization. This little town on the west bank of the Minnesota River was meant to be the fulfillment of the dreams of German romantics who wished to escape the debilitating rootlessness of urban life. The Turners felt that by settling on the soil they would create a natural haven where man's spiritual needs would be satisfied.

The Turner Movement in North America

In the period of nativist hostility and prejudice, the Turners defensively established a national headquarters (Turnerbund) in Cincinnati, and local Turnvereine in scores of cities. Early Turner city-founding ventures in the United States had been limited and exceptional until the Forty-Eighters came; but many refugee Forty-Eighters were eager to transplant the Turnverein in North America. Intellectuals and reformers, they retained the core of old world radicalism in the American Turnvereine, which were used by the Forty-Eighters as a vehicle for their political and social ideals.

In October, 1848, the first Turngemeinde in the United States was organized in Cincinnati when three Turners from Ludwigsburg arrived there and met Kienzel, a tavernkeeper and friend of Friedrich Hecker, who himself joined them shortly. Soon they had drawn up a constitution and bylaws, Hecker and his friends were joined by fourteen Cincinnati Germans, the group "erected a fence around an empty lot and began their physical exercises," and within two years they had built the first Turner Hall in the United States. The next year the society began to publish a monthly magazine. A century later, the society was still active.

Within a few years of the founding of the Cincinnati Turnverein, Turner societies sprang up in many of the larger cities — in Philadelphia, Baltimore, and New York, and westward to Chicago, Milwaukee, Davenport, St. Louis, and a host of smaller cities. By 1849 seventeen Turner societies existed in the United States, the number increasing to twenty-two by 1851, with a total membership of

1,672.[53] A year later, thirty societies took part in a Cincinnati gymnastic festival, and, largely as a result of the establishment of Turner schools — "to help the German immigrant . . . to become initiated into the American practices, to inculcate in them American ideals and to help them get an economic foothold in their adopted country"[54] — by the following year, 1854, the Turner movement had organized thirty-two more societies, bringing the total to sixty-two, with a combined membership of over 3,000.

Spurred by interest in the establishment of their own school system, the Turners spread across the United States, and by 1856 had organized Turnvereine in twenty-six states and the District of Columbia. The American Turnerbund report of that year revealed that total national membership had reached 5,995, organized in ten districts and eighty-two societies. Wilhelm Rapp, journalist on a number of German-American papers and editor of the *Turn-zeitung* (the official organ of the national organization) from 1855 to 1856, was president of the American Turnerbund for one term. Many others like Rapp — Sigismund Kaufmann, Eduard Müller, Wilhelm Rothacker, and Franz Sigel, to name a few — were political refugees of the 1848 Revolution who came to the United States and dedicated their lives to the ideals of the Turner movement — founding societies, editing Turner publications, lecturing for Turnerism, and giving instructions in physical education.[55]

So successful were the Turners in winning converts that by mid-century they were organized on a national scale. Having founded a union of gymnastic societies (Die Vereinigten Turnvereine Norda-

[53] Prahl, *op. cit.*, p. 99.

[54] *Turnerism Is Americanism*, compiled by Arthur A. Kuecken (Detroit. National Executive Committee of the American Turnerbund, 1938), pp. 6–7. In an earlier Turner catechism by Weier, *op. cit.*, p. 11, it is stated: "The Turner societies in the United States acted as Americanization agencies. All of them maintained night and Sunday schools, in which American history, American constitution and laws and other subjects were taught."

[55] Wittke, *Refugees*, p. 153. Some, like Müller, were extremists who wore the mantle of revolution throughout their lives: "His enthusiasm for his profession was so extraordinary that he became an eccentric figure. His daily costume was a white linen coat and trousers, which he wore, presumably, in emulation of Father Jahn; in the severest weather he refused to wear a vest, muffler, or overcoat, and his long gray locks hung down uncut over his shoulders."

marikas) in 1850 at a meeting of delegates in Philadelphia, the Turners began to exert a considerable influence among the middle classes in North America.[56] With national unity the Turners saw, in the next fifty years, the realization of many of their cherished ideas. At a convention in Buffalo in 1855 attended by representatives of forty-seven societies the Turnerbund adopted a platform which included two principles: "(1) The Turners are opposed to slavery and regard this institution as unworthy of a republic and not in accord with the principles of freedom. (2) The Turners are opposed to all prohibition laws as undemocratic in theory and not feasible in practice."[57] These principles, ahead of their time, invited attack from the forces favoring Negro slavery, who accused the Turners and all German-Americans of being alien-minded. The Turners' support of Abraham Lincoln, their refusal during the famous Baltimore riot to lower the Union flag from their hall, their formation of a personal bodyguard for Wendell Phillips, and their large-scale response to the call for Union volunteers[58] earned them a reputation among the pro-slavery groups as troublemakers, while focusing upon them the attention of the entire nation.

When the Civil War split the northern and southern sections of the Turnerbund, weakening their unity, vigorous countermeasures were taken by the national organization to strengthen the Turnerbund: the Turner Normal College at Indianapolis was established in 1865 to further the Turner education program; the first meeting of teachers of health and physical education in the history of American education was held in the same year at a Turnfest in Cincinnati. The Turners were largely responsible for the introduction of both physical education and the kindergarten into modern American public schools.

Despite their losses during the Civil War, the Turners increased

[56] Faust, *op. cit.*, Vol. II, p. 389. The name of the national society was changed the following year to Sozialistischer Turnerbund.

[57] Kuecken, *op. cit.*, p. 8.

[58] *Ibid.*, p. 13. Whole companies of Turners were formed; the 17th Missouri Regiment (known as the Western Turner Regiment) was made up almost entirely of Turners; twelve hundred Turners responded to a martial proclamation issued by the president of the New York Turner Society, serving under Colonel Max Weber. In all, 75 per cent of the American Turners enlisted in the Union Army.

their national membership from 9,300 in 1859 to 10,200 in 1867, reaching 12,000 by 1872, of whom 5,600 were active gymnasts. By 1876, total membership had climbed to nearly 14,000, in eighty-five clubs, with the property of the Turnerbund appraised at $1,854,222, of which approximately 40 per cent was encumbered by mortgages and other debts.[59]

Though the Civil War almost destroyed the movement, the excellent war record of the Turners helped reduce nativists' hostility toward them. Gradually the old revolutionary mood of the Turners faded, and the student romanticism of the early immigrants — the torchlight processions, songfests, public Turnfests, and militaristic parades — lapsed into memory. The Turnvereine became social organizations, devoted to recreation; in Hecker's words, they became a "gymnastic circus." Year by year the Turners relinquished their socialistic principles. When, in 1867, the executive committee organized an independent progressive party, the Turner membership felt it had gone too far, that its platform was too radical: "It called for 'impartial administration of justice without discrimination as to race, color, or nationality; uniform distribution of taxes; progressive capital and income tax; national support for the department of education; compulsory school education; that all monopolies be restricted and that the employee be protected against unjust demands of his employer.' "[60]

In marked contrast to their aims during the 1850's, by the 1870's the Turners had taken firm steps to de-politicize their organization, to extract all the teeth from the aging dragon of revolution. Turner Forty-Eighters would have been pleased to read the manifesto published in 1871, which declared: "We wish all men to be working men, sustaining themselves by the product of their labor, but by no means do we favor the creation of new class distinctions upon the overthrow of the present ruling class."[61] But with deep dismay the original Turners would have heard the statement issued by the national executive committee in 1872 to dispel charges that the Turners were alien-minded:

[59] Wittke, *Refugees*, p. 156.
[60] Kuecken, *op. cit.*, pp. 12–13.
[61] *Ibid.*, p. 13.

The Turners in America have nothing in common with the Turners of the old fatherland, except the system of health and physical education. Of our endeavors for reform in political, religious, and social fields, of the struggle against corruption and slavery in all forms, the Turners in Germany know nothing, although this has been the object and the inspiration of our Turnerbund.[62]

We now turn to an examination of the founding of Germania by a group of Turners, and its subsequent development and settlement by non-Turners, for further verification of the first hypothesis of this study concerning ethnic community formation, and for the unfolding of events which substantiate the second hypothesis that the shift to status community form is explainable both on the basis of the unusual status characteristics of the founding Turners and of their displacement by non-Turner German settlers of humbler origin.

[62] *Ibid.*, p. 13.

chapter 3

THE FOUNDING OF THE TOWN

GERMANIA, U.S.A., was founded at a time when Know-Nothingism was most intense; when Daniel Hertle, president of the Turnerbund in 1857, resolved that "the *Turner* [sic] are prepared to fight slavery, nativism, or any other deprivation of rights because of color, religion, place of birth, or sex, since such attitudes are not compatible with a cosmopolitan *Weltanschauung.*"[1] In response to outside pressures, and acting in accordance with their own utopian ideals, the Turners organized a colonization society to aid Turners and their friends to find good sites on which to settle and build a life of their own.[2] In discussing the founding of Germania, Mrs. Johnson observes that one of the aims of the founders was "to establish a community where the liberal principles of the *Turner* could be followed by German immigrants, unhampered by interference from Know-Nothing mobs or by restrictions through Blue Laws. Such a congenial atmosphere was realized in this town with its population of more than 80 per cent German."[3]

Germania was a pioneer enterprise set in motion by one of the original members of the Cincinnati Turnverein, William Pfaender, who "conceived the idea of a settlement of workers and free-thinkers in the Northwest where good soil and lumber were abundant, where

[1] Zucker, in Zucker, *op. cit.*, p. 303.
[2] Prahl, in Zucker, *op. cit.*, p. 96.
[3] Hildegard Binder Johnson, "Adjustment to the United States," in Zucker, *op. cit.*, p. 74.

53

each family could have its garden plot, and where a socialistic society by means of public ownership could flourish, free from the evils of unemployment and want."[4] Pfaender and another Forty-Eighter, Jacob Nix, proposed the idea at the Turners' annual convention in Buffalo in 1855. Financial support was forthcoming from the Western groups, particularly the Cincinnati Turners (the Eastern societies declining to back so unfeasible a venture), and Pfaender was elected to draft the charter of the Settlement Society of the Socialistic Turnerbund.[5] Though the Turner colonization society was not unique — many immigrant groups of the 1850's launched similar ventures — the Turnvereine were unusually active in promoting these enterprises. Moreover, the Turners' aim to colonize the American West by wedding "practical gymnastics" to socialistic organization was unique.

Pfaender, one of the more energetic, idealistic Turners, had a guiding hand in the organization of the Turngemeinde in Heilbronn, the Cincinnati Turngemeinde a few years later, and finally the Turnverein and the town of Germania. He published an article, "Praktisches Turnen," in which he claimed that true security could be gained only in masses; the individual would strive for it in vain.[6]

[4] *Ibid.*, pp. 71–72.

[5] Also called the "Colonization Society of North America," and the "Turner Colonization Society of Cincinnati." The charter was drafted at a special convention on January 20, 1856. The European socialist heritage of early American Turnerism is evident in its formal statement, "General Principles of the American Gymnastic Union," published by the Society's National Executive Committee in 1919 (Weier, *op. cit.*, p. 26): "If economic conditions are such as to produce extremes like the millionaire and the pauper, the centralization of political power in certain classes becomes inevitable. For these reasons we endorse efforts tending to equalize conditions in our economic life." And cautiously but more explicitly in the next paragraph: "We favor social institutions and legal enactments which will check the exploitation of labor by capital; have a tendency to secure to the worker the fruits of his labor; prevent wrongs and injustice in the struggles between capital and labor and give the development of our economic conditions a direction toward abolition of all class distinctions."

[6] Published in the March 29, 1855, issue of the *Turn Zeitung* of Philadelphia, official organ of the Nordamerikanischer Turnerbund. The Turner creed is inconsistent as to which is more important, the individual or the collective. One Turner catechism, for example, states (Weier, *op. cit.*, p. 18): "Participants in military drill are part of a collective unit and lose their individuality. (. . . school boys should not be given military drill.)" Four pages later one finds the "altruistic" nature and "communal benefits" of

Writing at a time when public feeling against the social habits of freethinkers and Turners was intense, and when the expansion of the Turnerbund offered hope for many, Pfaender's ideas had great attraction for many German immigrants. The disheartening 1850's, a time of economic distress and unemployment in North America, inspired many immigrant workmen to seek a new start at the edge of the frontier, "beyond the reach of greedy land speculators," where they might "obtain government land and create a model town, which should be surrounded by gardens."[7] A group of German workmen from Chicago, driven by this motive, were already platting the town-site of Germania when Pfaender arrived at the end of his long search.

Settlement by the Chicago Land Verein. Pfaender was thus not the first to propose a settlement on the present site of Germania. The Turners had been preceded by Ferdinand Beinhorn from Braunschweig by way of Chicago. Beinhorn had conceived this idea of establishing a settlement of equals, a German frontier colony far removed from the dangers and pitfalls of city life.

Shortly after his arrival in New York in 1852, and even before he reached Milwaukee, Beinhorn had intended to found a German colony in the American Middle West. After experienced friends dissuaded him from attempting a utopian community project, Beinhorn first decided "to buy a few sections of government land, establish a city, divide it into lots, and then push these lots on the market."[8] Soon after, however, in 1853, Beinhorn met six German workmen studying English at an evening class in Chicago and per-

Turner physical training extolled, as compared with the "egoistic" purposes of other athletic societies, which benefit the individual at the expense of the group: "The Athletic Club trains the individual, the Turners train the masses." It would seem that gymnastics had for the Turners none of the painful connotations of military discipline, which historically had meant their defeat before superior Prussian forces. However, the Turners habitually formed drill companies in nineteenth-century America, an inconsistency far less in evidence by the turn of the century.

[7] L. A. Fritsche, *History of Brown County, Minnesota*, Vol. I (Indianapolis: B. F. Bowen & Co., 1916), p. 124. This quotation, like much of the material in Fritsche's *History*, is originally from the more authoritative account by Edward D. Neill, *History of the Minnesota Valley* (Minneapolis: North Star Publishing Co., 1882), p. 704.

[8] *New Ulm Daily Journal*, June 26, 1962, p. 2. Article by Hildegard Binder Johnson.

suaded them to unite with him in searching for a townsite "where all could find independence and establish a heritage for their children."[9]

Soon joined by a dozen friends and acquaintances, Beinhorn and these six workmen gathered in the late summer of 1853 to organize the Chicago Land Verein, and agreed to accept "every person of good character." Meetings were held every week, and the membership increased to sixty by November, 1853, eight hundred by April, 1854, less than a year after the first meeting of the Society. Nearly all members were working men, inspired by the prospect of founding their own community. As winter passed and plans were impatiently reviewed, the members became more and more eager to leave Chicago, which was "a miserable slough," so poor in sanitation that hundreds succumbed that year to cholera.[10]

Grown too large to convene at the home of one of the original members, the Society moved its meetings to Chicago's Turner Hall, where they sponsored a ball to raise funds for the project which netted $300. A monthly payment of $.10 a member to meet expenses was supplanted by an initiation fee of $3 plus an assessment of $5. Thus supplied with funds to purchase land, the Society sent out committees in the spring of 1854 to scout newly opened territory, cautioning them to select a tract with ample timber located on a navigable river. Sites were explored in Michigan, Iowa, and Missouri. An unscrupulous land agent, hoping for a quick profit, chartered a steamboat for an expedition to the sand dunes of northern Michigan.[11] Finally, in the summer of 1854, agents investigating the frontier in southern Minnesota, a comparatively virgin area of twenty-four million acres, returned with favorable accounts of this region recently evacuated by the Sioux.

Though some members were unwilling to go so far into the wilder-

[9] Evan Jones, *The Minnesota: Forgotten River* (New York: Holt, Rinehart, and Winston, 1962), p. 153.

[10] *Ibid.*, pp. 153–154.

[11] *Ibid.* Jones remarks about this incident: "Beinhorn must have been furious. He had grown up distrusting Hanoverian landowners, and now in America, where he counted on justice and freedom, he had been faced with duplicity that could be considered nothing but despicable." See also Neill, *op. cit.*, p. 704.

ness — so close to Indian reservations — most were ready at last to have their association become a town. At the end of September, an advance party of twenty-three men, eight of them married and accompanied by their wives and children, set out for the promised land, journeying up the Mississippi to St. Paul and from there to Le Sueur.[12] Two likely locations were looked at only to be abandoned. With a winter crispness in the morning air, and no good townsite available, some of the party began to feel that their mission was futile.[13] While four volunteered to continue the search westward, the rest remained temporarily at Traverse des Sioux, in a hotel operated by a German.

The four trailblazers from Chicago, familiar only with the outdoors of the old country, followed paths leading to Fort Ridgley, an outpost against the Indians, hoping to encounter someone who could direct them to a site they had heard of in the region below the fort and along the river. Finally, that night, guided by flashes of lightning, they chanced upon the trading post of Joseph La Framboise, who took them into his house, offered them muskrat meat, and passed around his favorite calumet. A veteran trader who had lived in the district for a quarter of a century, La Framboise told them of a location he considered superior to any other in the whole valley, a site known to voyageurs as Prairie Belle View. Germania, U.S.A., was born.

The next day, returning to Traverse des Sioux from a visit to the site armed with glowing reports of its natural beauty and excellent possibilities — with its "wide bench-like plateaus rising gradually and stretching along the valley several miles, like the tiers of an

[12] There are conflicting reports of the present account: five semi-independent accounts of the situation vary the number of advance settlers from twenty to twenty-three to thirty and thirty-two. The earliest settlers left Chicago in small groups, assembling at St. Paul to await the final selection of a site by the advance party. On September 26, 1854, the entire group left St. Paul for Le Sueur, a trip of seventy-odd miles, traveling mainly by steamboat, but also by ox team and on horseback.

[13] A report in the *Brown County Historical Society Bulletin*, New Ulm, 1962, notes that the inadequacy of the Le Sueur region for a townsite was met with bitter disappointment and dissension which for a time "threatened to wreck the whole enterprise." These were cautious men, unwilling to gamble against improbable odds.

enormous amphitheater"[14] — the four German burghers led the party left there to the townsite. The date of their arrival was October 8, 1854. As the lateness of the season prevented them from erecting houses before cold weather set in, they went to a point eleven miles from Prairie Belle View where, joined by more settlers from Chicago, they spent a hard winter in the flimsy lodges of an abandoned Indian village, freezing and nearly starving. An early spring brought relief, and all except one survived the ordeal.

With spring and after some argument over the best location for the new town — finally resolved in Chicago — the group was joined in May, 1855, by twenty members of the Chicago Society who had originally come from the village of Erbach in Wurtemberg.[15] Most were Swabians. Among them was Volk, who, following instructions from President Beinhorn, laid out the original townsite. The townsmen laid claim to the land and formally dedicated the site, naming it New Ulm after Ulm, Germany. The first structure on the actual townsite, a crude fourteen-by-sixteen foot log cabin named the Courthaus, built to secure the claim, was soon surrounded by a scattering of temporary houses, some made of sod.

By the summer of 1855 these temporary dwellings had been replaced by more permanent log cabins, in all twenty-three houses and their outbuildings. It was the only settlement for miles around. The new sawmill was ripping logs from dawn until dusk, land-clearing and cultivating advanced apace, mail arrived with increasing regularity, and Fred Roebecke was operating the community's first store, which boasted an inventory including "30 pounds of coffee, half a barrel of sugar, one barrel of salt, 5 bolts of cotton goods, and half a barrel of whiskey."[16] Food was scarce and expensive: beef sold for $.20 a pound, butter from $.35 to $.40, potatoes for $2.00 a bushel — and a barrel of flour, when available, for $20.00. Cornmeal was the chief food, and even in 1857 there was very little flour or pork. Many families took to roasting corn and peas as a substitute for coffee.

[14] Jones, *op. cit.*, p. 156.

[15] From a speech by Colonel William Pfaender, first president of New Ulm, on the fiftieth anniversary of the settlement, held at the Turner theater in 1904 under the auspices of the Junior Pioneer Society.

[16] *Brown County Historical Society Bulletin* 1962, no pages.

By early summer, 1856, the young community was a qualified success, but it was also in trouble. Though the land association had taken the first steps toward acquiring the land a year before, actual filings were not made until the spring of 1856, when only 320 acres could be pre-empted for townsite purposes. This was far too limited an area for Beinhorn's dream. Funds to buy 2,200 acres more of the land surrounding the townsite were raised by assessing each member $30, in return for which he was to receive twelve town lots and 9 acres of garden tract. Those who failed to pay the amount in four weeks' time would forfeit their membership in the association. Two hundred and fifty men paid.[17]

At an excited gathering of the Society in Chicago, President Beinhorn collected the money received, prepared to make the necessary payments to secure sixteen quarter sections of land, and delivered it to treasurer Albert Blatz, a brother of the prominent Milwaukee brewer, Valentine Blatz. Both set out at once for New Ulm, arriving in May to register as much land as they could afford. But they did not have enough to pay the land-office fees for all the acreage that Beinhorn wanted for his colony. The community's financial difficulties were pressing in May, 1856, when Beinhorn met "a stranger strolling curiously among the new houses and surveyor's stakes."[18] That meeting with Pfaender changed the fate of Germania.

The Arrival of the Turners

Had Pfaender not arrived, "it is quite possible that the history of New Ulm might have ended during that summer."[19] As the emissary of the Colonization Society of North America, Pfaender came with money in his pocket, ready to put "practical gymnastics" into practice — the Turnzeitung's phrase for a Turner pioneer settlement. He quickly grasped the fact that Beinhorn was having financial difficulties, and made known his mission. Though Pfaender's group, more philosophic and radical than Beinhorn's, intended to bring a socialistic community to the prairies, whereas Beinhorn's was mainly

[17] Neill, *op. cit.*, p. 705.
[18] Jones, *op. cit.*, p. 158.
[19] *New Ulm Daily Journal*, June 26, 1962, p. 2.

interested in better homes, both were looking for essentially the same thing, and they decided to merge. Renaming their new joint enterprise the German Land Association of Minnesota, incorporated by an act of the legislature and approved on March 4, 1857, they proclaimed that their object was "to procure a home for every German laborer, popish priests and lawyers excepted, in some healthy and productive district, located on some navigable river." [20]

The Turners lost no time in revitalizing the struggling community. Actually, they were the ones who formally established it. For months they had been selling shares to Germans throughout the United States to finance such a venture. Pfaender and two associates had searched for a townsite in Missouri, Iowa, Kansas, and Nebraska, when they learned of the Chicago Germans' attempts to build a community in the valley. Backed by the Cincinnati Turnverein and intending to acquire land "in a healthy region" that would "offer good trade facilities," Pfaender found exactly what he was looking for in New Ulm. Having sold members eight hundred shares at $15 each until May 1, 1856, for $20 each until July 1, and for $25 each after that date, the Turner group was in excellent financial condition.[21] They received an additional $3,000 from the Cincinnati Turnverein to buy supplies to carry them through the winter.

The German Land Association became the new owner of New Ulm on July 4, 1856, when the Beinhorn group sold its holdings to the Turner Colonization Society for about $6,000.[22] Under the terms of the agreement, the Cincinnati company offered to build a community sawmill, warehouse, and flourmill. It was decided that the Chicago society should be refunded the amount they had paid for the land. The Turners were favored by the fact that the members of the Chicago society had platted but not yet located on the site of New Ulm. The Turners achieved amalgamation free of established settlement patterns, and immediately began to modify the original scheme to conform with their own.

The original distribution of lots and garden holdings was

[20] Fritsche, *op. cit.,* p. 466.

[21] *New Ulm Daily Journal,* June 26, 1962, p. 8; also Johnson, in Zucker, *op. cit.,* p. 72.

[22] Each of the two hundred members of the Chicago society was to receive $33 in cash.

changed.[23] By the new apportionment each member of the Chicago society, formerly promised twelve lots and nine acres of garden land outside, received six lots and four acres, while the Cincinnati people were to hold three lots and four acres. Lots were offered for sale to non-members at $50 each.

With this agreement, Pfaender, back from Chicago where he had negotiated the merger of the two companies, obtained an additional tract of sixteen quarter sections of land from the government. In August he reported to a special convention in Cincinnati that he had bought in all from the Chicago company, 4,836 acres of land — 1,700 acres open townsite land, the rest partly timbered. Pfaender also bought a claim bordering the river — where he feared a rival settlement might otherwise develop — a strip of land about seven miles wide and eight miles long. Thus the land association was generously supplied, and some 9,000 acres of good prairie land still vacant, much of it worth from $200 to $400 an acre in 1965, was distributed among the various claims of the association.[24] Pfaender recommended an amendment to the constitution urging each member to help himself to farmland and to lay claim to a quarter section among the four hundred choice tracts still available in the neighborhood.

When the land association was incorporated in 1857, the capital stock was fixed at $100,000, each share valued at $50. Firm strides were taken to establish a thriving community. The association was "authorized to erect . . . buildings, mills, and other structures, together with steam engines, and all the machinery necessary for the manufacture of lumber, flour, machinery, agricultural implements, cotton and woolen goods, paper, and all such articles adapted to the wants of the country, as shall be deemed best by the stockholders."[25]

[23] The Turners had envisioned a kind of truck-garden community, a "gardenland." Land was to be distributed by lottery, no one was to hold more than two shares. Each share entitled the holder to one town lot, and a small garden outside the townsite. Those wishing to engage in agriculture could be assured of more land at cost price. City property was restricted to one sharelot, one hundred acres of garden land.

[24] Beinhorn and sixteen claimants had bought the land in 1856 at the government price, $1.25 an acre.

[25] Neill, *op. cit.*, p. 707.

Careful plans were laid to enable Germania to grow without suffering the overcrowding its members had known in large European and American cities. In the late spring of 1857 Christian Prignitz platted the huge tract incorporated as New Ulm and filed in April, 1858.[26] The vision of the planners was grand: it was "perhaps the most remarkable townsite plat ever made on a new frontier,"[27] engineered, "planned to the last detail, as Pierre Charles L'Enfant had planned Washington, D.C." observes Jones, adding:

Christian Prignitz . . . had a glowing vision of his city's future. The bearded, blue-eyed young German saw rising above the river a community that one day would have from seventy-five thousand to one hundred thousand inhabitants. His design allowed no possibility of the usual speculators' subdivisions joined together in helter-skelter fashion. His city was completely platted on nearly six thousand acres of glacial bench. . . . Young Prignitz drew no grand diagonal avenues like those of the national capital, but he laid out the distinguished parks that exist in New Ulm today, and bisected his plan with one broad, handsomely landscaped boulevard. . . . his design has survived every stage through which New Ulm has grown.[28]

The Failure of Socialism

No less ambitious and carefully worked out were the socialistic plans of the Turner group, who at first enjoyed financial and perhaps numerical superiority in Germania. Their scheme was more grand and utopian than that of the Chicago group: the Turners intended to see communal ownership made profitable. Success seemed certain.

With some thirteen hundred members in 1856, the Cincinnati society was able to contribute in the first year of joint settlement proportionately more money and men to the experimental community than could the Chicago society, which by the same year had

[26] The subject of a name for the newly incorporated community came up again. No fewer than eighteen were proposed at the Cincinnati convention, the most extraordinary of which were Nibelungen, Thusnelda, Sparta, and Hutten, the last most favored. However, the settlers of New Ulm ignored these suggestions and kept the original name given by the Chicago group.

[27] Brown County Historical Society report, 1962.

[28] Jones, *op. cit.*, p. 159.

declined to about two hundred members. While the population of New Ulm in 1854 was about thirty, all original settlers from Chicago, to which were added in the year following some twenty more members of the society, by 1856 the arrival of the Turners boosted the population to well over a hundred, most being from Cincinnati. In 1857 sixty to seventy more families[29] arrived from Cincinnati, bringing the total to three hundred and fifty-six. Germania's future was assured.

The crystalline vision of the Turners shattered under the hard demands of the American frontier. Utopia in any guise was not easily sustained in the region "ultra limites militares,"[30] a lesson the townsmen quickly learned. There was Lebensraum to spare in Germania, and expansiveness was the mood of the day. But the Turners needed more than ideas, more than a passion for freedom and equality, to make their community a success. Once the land had been bought and paid for, the burgeoning socialistic community found itself desperately short of funds.

The Association's communal business enterprises were uniformly unsuccessful. Pfaender, elected first president of the Association in 1857, took over the management of the unfinished sawmill from the Land Society, completed it in 1857, and saw it $4,000 in debt by 1858. Sharp criticism by the townsmen of this unprofitable venture led to an unsuccessful attempt to sell it for $6,000; it was then rented out and run as a private enterprise, and finally sold in 1862, the money going to pay the outstanding debt. The shareholders lost most of their investment in this first socialistic enterprise. Similar problems arose with other communal ventures.

The Association was forced to sell the community warehouse as

---

[29] *New Ulm Daily Journal*, June 26, 1962, p. 4, claims that "in the spring of 1857 the steamboat, *Frank Steele*, brought 70 families from Cincinnati on one trip." There are no reliable population figures available for the years before 1857, when the first census was taken. Estimates of the 1854 population vary, and no firm figure can be found for 1856. The guess made for 1856 is based on the difference between the known 1855 and 1857 populations, which showed an increase of approximately 300 during that period.

[30] One descendant of the pioneer settlers pointed out that in the early days New Ulm was said to lie "beyond the military border." It had been the ambition of many Turners in Metternich's day to journey beyond the military borders of Prussia.

early as 1857; its Globe Mill was not competitive with Old Schramm's wind grist mill, and another community-owned enterprise, the *New Ulm Pioneer*, a four-page weekly newspaper established in 1858, after struggling for lack of funds and paper to "proclaim and propagate the radical principles of the Colonization Association," was sold to its salaried editor a year later.[31]

The town council met weekly to discuss the sale and distribution of shares, the assignment of lots, the transfer of deeds, and other business. They could do little, however, to control the mounting crisis in communal ownership which was quickened by the influx of settlers. Pfaender had been put in charge of the communal store, which sold to all the inhabitants at cost. Its limited stock rapidly dwindled as the new arrivals overtaxed the supply; many of the newcomers, arriving after a long and costly journey, had little money or supplies.[32] As the nearest source of foodstuffs and hard goods was a hundred and twenty miles away, the whole distance over bad roads and unbridged streams, prices in Germania rose once again. Enormous prices were charged in 1858 for staple commodities: a barrel of flour went for $22; potatoes for $3.00 a bushel; chickens sold for $5.00 each; and a cat which, it is said, some enterprising individual had bought to alleviate the mouse problem, was rented out at $2.00 per customer.[33]

Attempts to raise a wheat crop in 1856 and 1857 failed. Blackbirds found the wheat crop the second year; a prairie fire left it in ashes the third, when an excellent crop promised the settlers relief from their drab staple of cornmeal. Many of the early settlers were workmen, tradesmen, and artisans — urban types, not farmers. They had little talent or taste for tilling the soil. Some lived in rude huts or dugouts; a man named Haeberle was obliged to dig up his spring seed potatoes to feed his family. Luxuries were few; the little available tobacco did not go far, and most men smoked leaves and chewed roots from the forest. Such conditions prevailed in New Ulm and

[31] Interview with a first-generation Turner, 1962. The *Pioneer* was set up with two pages printed in German, two in English.

[32] In those days, one informant relates, a man with money (more than $100) was rare. A team of oxen cost from $200 to $240.

[33] Fritsche, *op. cit.*, pp. 139–140.

vicinity for five to eight years, after which the community became self-sustaining, soon to emerge as a major trading center serving a wide region.

Faced with these vexing problems and impatient for the good life, the town council — consisting of the Turner president, Pfaender, and non-Turners Beinhorn and two associates, Henry Meyerding and Hermann Herrendorfer — invited the shareholders to a general assembly of the German Land Association in 1858 to discuss the socialistic tendencies of the Turnerbund, which almost all disapproved of, and of Germania, which most found unsatisfactory. Though further community projects were suggested, such as a quarry, a cemetery, a public sand and clay kiln, warehouses, the municipal sale of liquor, and the purchase of agricultural machinery, the Association had no money to finance any of these projects. It was pointed out at another meeting a month later that "a settlement of poor people could not thrive unless families with means also settled and provided opportunities for others." [34]

By December, 1858, the capital assets of the Association had dwindled to $7,400, and its debts mounted precipitately. The Cincinnati Turnverein became alarmed over Germania's financial embarrassment, accusing the settlers of speculation and mismanagement. Shareholders began to demand detailed financial reports from the Association, threatening to withdraw their support. In May, 1859, the situation crystallized into the only form possible: the German Land Association dissolved, deeding its schoolhouse with inventory and twenty-four building lots to the New Ulm school district, to which they subsequently bequeathed $5,594.25 in cash and three hundred and twenty additional lots. The shareholders lost their investments. The Turnverein, leaders in education, received $400 from the Association to build an addition onto their hall for use by the public schools, the use of which the schools had enjoyed free of charge since the first classes were held in the Turner Hall.

This turn of events altered the nature of education in Germania as well as the influence of the Turners in religious matters, from the beginning a subject of acute concern to freethinkers and church-

[34] *New Ulm Daily Journal*, June 26, 1962, p. 2.

goers alike. The dream of President and Active Chairman Pfaender, who worked for the realization of "a German settlement, avoidance of speculation, educational opportunities for the children of liberals and freethinkers,"[35] expresses the Turners' point of view. It was not until 1862 that the Association brought its business affairs to a close, establishing a permanent school fund with more than $4,000 received from the auction of the remaining land. The Turners were successful in keeping religion out of the public school system by stipulating that under the terms of the education fund no religious instruction should be given in New Ulm's public schools, and no Bibles should be found in their libraries.[36]

In short, by 1859 socialism had been abandoned in Germania.

Turnerism and Germania's Growth

By the end of the first winter, twenty-three houses had been built in Germania. After less than five years had passed, by 1860, one hundred and eighty buildings had been erected. The first edition of the *New Ulm Pioneer*, dated January 1, 1858, reported that the town had ninety-five buildings on its fifty-nine hundred lots, of which six were general stores, one a woolen piece-goods store, two blacksmith shops, one a butcher shop, and two flourmills. With a population of over four hundred, served by three doctors but no lawyers or clergymen, surrounded by four hundred ninety-three four-acre outlots, and operating a brewery and a Turner Hall, Germania, U.S.A., was thriving.

The growing families of the earliest settlers, most of whom were in their twenties and thirties, quickly created a need for schools. Simultaneously with the incorporation of the town in 1857, the first school was completed, supplies were procured, and the teacher, August Westphal, was hired for $40 a month by the German Land Association. He gave instruction in German to twenty-four of New Ulm's fifty children. The next year saw a one hundred per cent

[35] *Ibid.*, p. 2.
[36] *Ibid.* The first of these conditions persists today. A gentleman's agreement was reached as a result of the growth of the Roman Catholic and Lutheran population in New Ulm; the six-member school board traditionally has two freethinkers, two Roman Catholics and two Protestants.

increase in the school population (to one hundred and five), and thirty-five newborn. Sixty-one students were in school when the Association dissolved. (A century later the New Ulm school population had increased approximately sixty times.)

In the brief period of ethnic consolidation, the Turners achieved their immediate aims. The interpretation of their achievements by Robert Schlinkert, resident priest of Germania's first Roman Catholic church, is revealing: "Because of their overwhelming numbers, they [the Turners] had great influence in matters of school and town government. This fact also caused considerable friction between the so-called free-thinkers and the church people. Nevertheless, the settlement continued to make rapid headway." [37] Schlinkert observed that New Ulm "originated with a society of German immigrants composed largely of freethinkers dominated by socialistic and anti-clerical elements." [38] The Reverend Alexander Schwinn elaborates this: when Father Berghold first came to Germania in December, 1868, a hotel proprietor told him he was wasting his time, since Germania "was not interested in religion." In fact, Schwinn goes on, "many citizens influenced by the Turner Society of that day were opposed to churches of all denominations." When Father Berghold asked the hotelkeeper for the names of the Catholics in the town, "he could enumerate only twelve families of reliable Catholics." [39] Meanwhile, from 1856 to 1869, the year Father Berghold established the first Roman Catholic church, Holy Trinity parish, within the city limits, Germania remained a Turner village. It was not until the completion of Holy Trinity Church in 1905, when New Ulm was portrayed by Father Schlinkert as a "center of Catholicity," that the eclipse of the Turner element became obvious to all. [40]

[37] *The Holy Trinity Church of Germania, Minnesota: A Record of 75 Years (1869–1944)*, trans. by Alphonse J. Matt (New Ulm: privately printed, 1944; first printing, 1919), pp. 12–13.

[38] *Ibid.*, p. 19.

[39] *A History of the Church of St. George of West Newton, Minnesota: 1858–1958* (New Ulm and Mankato: privately printed, 1958), p. 42.

[40] The rise of Roman Catholicism, and religion generally, was not fully appreciated by all. As early as 1858 the *New Ulm Pioneer*, organ of the Turner Land Association, declared: "Many want all church humbug ban-

Contention and Change

The year 1859 marked a turning point in the history of Germania and in the role of the Turners there. Though they retained their initial dominance in town life for several decades thereafter, they ceased to be its main component. With the dissolution of the Association, the aims of the Turners could no longer be legally instituted. Their radical economics could not cope with frontier realities, while the steady inflow of non-Turners whose religious and political beliefs were opposed to Turner atheism and liberalism was the decisive force that hastened the decline of Turner control.[41]

Between 1856 and the 1870's the Turners had built their first hall — in 1858 one of the most impressive structures in town and even in 1890 still the city's chief place of amusement — and emerged as the social and political leaders of the community.[42] From the first the central institution in the lives of the settlers, the Turnverein as late as 1900 remained "by all odds the most powerful [society] in the city." Organized in 1856 with a membership of thirteen, it held the town's first theatrical presentation of the German plays, *Einer*

ished, others believe to strike out the church is necessary. We are absolutely inclined to the latter opinion." And in less uncertain terms, it added, "The Bible, a mixture of moral truth, moral falsehood, and natural scientific lies . . . is absolutely unfit for scholastic instruction." *New Ulm Pioneer*, 1858, No. 1 (trans. by Mrs. William Durbahn), pp. 2, 3.

[41] It would be a mistake to explain the failure of socialism in Germania solely in economic terms. Under the Turners, Germania, as an experiment in communal living, differed markedly from many of the utopian communities in North America during the mid-nineteenth century. The religious communism of Oneida, for instance, was not practiced in Germania, whose Turner leaders were antireligious. The identification of Turnerism with atheism led to a rift between the religious and non-religious elements of the early community which spelled the eclipse of socialism partly for non-economic reasons. (In this regard, Charles Nordholl, a careful student of utopian communities in nineteenth century North America, concluded that while the Germans made better communists than any other people, a commune could only succeed when composed of persons who shared some common religious beliefs.) Despite the economic advantages of communal living, in addition to its attractive social equality, Germania's experience indicates that the first consideration may well have been religious or ideological.

[42] Three Turner halls were built, the first in 1857 and destroyed by fire in 1862; the second in 1866, damaged by a cyclone in 1881 and razed in 1900; the third in 1901, at a cost of $25,000, was gutted by fire in 1952 and rebuilt immediately.

Muss Heiraten (One Must Marry) and *Die Tochter Pharonis* (The Daughter of Pharonis), in the year of its completion.[43] In the early days the Turnverein served as Germania's town hall. Its doors were open for a host of events. In 1857 the townspeople held their first Christmas celebration in the Turner Hall, and the Turners themselves conducted their own Sunday school classes there. Concerts, lectures, gymnastic festivals, banquets and dances, school meetings and law sessions — all these occupied its stage, social hall, dining room, and gymnasium. The official history of the New Ulm Turnverein recounts that the new hall became the center for the whole community, and that "the meetings of the *Verein* often developed into a general one of all citizens, and then many public affairs were discussed." [44]

Decline and Ascent among Germania's Turners

Germania is today a thriving Midwest trading and manufacturing center set among beds of gravel and silt and lying near the junction of one of the world's greatest rivers with a smaller stream. Flanked by headlands rising steeply on the east and west, headlands carved by the river and softened by eons of rain and advancing vegetation, the valley in which Germania lies had for thousands of years remained little changed by the Indian's timeless tread and silent arrow. Then came the settlers, whose axe and saw shattered the stillness of centuries; whose plow turned the virgin soil; whose houses, streets, mills, and factories quickly erased all but memories of the past. Even the stars go unseen within the glare of the electric arc lamp.

The land was claimed and its fertility released to sustain a new way of life brought by these strangers, wrapped in dreams that were reflected in their searching eyes. Fleeing a society wrenched by the upheavals of burgeoning nationhood, they brought to North America a culture plucked from the storms of revolution. They found a land quite different from their own, a land unsettled and changing,

[43] Edward Petry, *The First Fifty Years* (New Ulm: privately printed, trans. by Minnie Loenholt, 1956), p. 5.
[44] *Ibid.*, p. 5.

where frontiers awaited discovery and where experiment was the shortest road to success. Beset by the events of recent years in Europe and under the fire of nativists who had barely preceded them to the United States, immigrants from Swabia, Württemberg, Baden, Westphalia, and Bavaria hurried westward from city to city, arriving in Minnesota Territory a century ago to gaze hopefully at an uncharted life.

Turner and non-Turner they came, at first a trickle, then in a rush, to their new fatherland, to Germania, a hybrid transplant which they nurtured and made endure, its roots anchored deep in frontier soil, its broad branches giving them protection and comfort in their semi-isolation. But they could not for long remain a little Bavaria.

At the same time that the Turners were strengthening their organization, various members and officers of the Turnverein moved into positions of leadership in the community. Though they monopolized the key positions in the early years, soon they were challenged by "outsiders" who were not content to remain excluded from significant participation in town government, education, civic affairs, and the like. Since 1857 Germania has been governed by eight different kinds of municipal rule; in each the Turners have been active in greater proportion than their numbers would seem to justify. Yet in each decade they have increasingly shared the responsibilities of self-government (realized in 1876) with non-Turners. Turner leadership in Germania's municipal affairs was never so complete as during the first twenty years, when Pfaender was president, when, in 1862, Turners Charles Roos and Jacob Nix led the town in defense against the Sioux Indian attack, Roos acting as sheriff and Nix as commander of the engagement, or when these men were, respectively, the first mayor and clerk of the newly incorporated borough (1876).

With the failure of socialism in Germania the core of the Turner ideal dissolved. The rise and consolidation of religiously and economically "alien" elements in the community brought to a close the brief period of undisputed Turner leadership. The new phase in the social history of the Germania Turners, after their decline as a dominant ethnic group, may be called the period of status ascension.

It is to this post-ethnic period that we now turn, using data contained not only in historical accounts but also in the questionnaire schedules used as a basis for this book. As predicted, the emergence of the Germania Turnverein as an upper status group was the logical outcome of their displacement by non-Turner immigrants.

III

Class, Status, and Power

chapter 4

CLASS AND CHALLENGE

MY SECOND general hypothesis maintains that forces intrinsic to the Turner ethnic community account for its becoming a status sub-community. It will be tested by contrasting first and second generations of Turners and non-Turners with respect to predicted changes in the four dimensions of class, status, power, and assimilation. Descriptive data from the research instrument and from historical sources bearing on these hypotheses will be presented before a statistical analysis of differences, in which the scale results will form the conclusive test of each working hypothesis, is made.

Class

The theoretical basis for the concepts of class, status, and power as employed in this book is the famous essay by Max Weber.[1] It has been noted that his theory of stratification is distinctive in two ways: first, he isolated three categories of social activity (power, esteem, and wealth); second, he found that these are advanced through three types of social groups (parties, status groups, and classes).[2] Briefly, a class is a number of persons sharing an equivalent access in a market economy to the wealth of their society. A hierarchy of

[1] "Class, Status, Party," in *From Max Weber: Essays in Sociology*, trans. and ed., with an introduction by H. H. Gerth and C. Wright Mills (New York: Oxford University Press, 1958), pp. 180–195.

[2] The interpretation of Weber's theory given here follows in part that presented by Martindale, *American Social Structure*, pp. 448–450. Warner's concept of "social class" (see Warner, Meeker, and Eels, *op. cit.*) represents,

classes, built on unequal lines of access to wealth, is the economic part of the social order.[3] Two basic categories of class situation, observed Weber, are thus property and lack of property.[4] Today, however, class is less determined by property than it was in Weber's time. The class situation of the majority of Americans, for example — of executives, professional people, and managers as well as clerical workers and laborers — is largely administered. The day of the independent entrepreneur is past. It is therefore more accurate to say that class is now determined primarily by the degree of access to economic opportunities.[5]

in my view, a confusion of meaningful social reality. Warner distorts the nature of social stratification, robs it of its full meaning by fusing class and status. This makes wealth and prestige count as the same, resulting, for example, in the peculiar expedient of rating both a wealthy but disreputable implement dealer and an impoverished schoolteacher of old family heritage as middle-middle. This technique of rating individuals by social class is ill suited for revealing the social significance of class as compared to status. As everyone knows, whether a man has immense wealth and great prestige or immense wealth but no prestige, may make all the difference in his life. Surely, the campaign to refashion the public's image of John D. Rockefeller was launched out of a shrewd realization of the importance of this difference.

[3] Gerth and Mills, *op. cit.*, pp. 181, 194. The economic order is not identical with the social order, though the two influence one another. "The economic order is . . . merely the way in which economic goods and services are distributed and used." The relation of the economic and social order of class and status is seen by Weber as follows: "Whereas the genuine place of 'classes' is within the economic order, the place of 'status groups' is within the social order, that is, within the sphere of the distribution of 'honor.' "

Weber's distinction reflects the nineteenth-century idea that class relations are fundamentally economic and are to be understood in Western market terms. Indeed they are, though only in Western societies; but even as applied to market societies a rigid analytical separation of the economic from the social and political may lead to the specious conclusion that human motives are unidimensional, or can be understood as if they were, as is implied by terms like "class behavior" and "class consciousness."

[4] *Ibid.*, p. 182.

[5] Evidence requiring this shift in the meaning of class is abundant; a notable discussion of the decline of the small entrepreneur and the rise of a new propertyless middle class in American society is C. Wright Mills's *White Collar* (New York: Oxford University Press, 1953), pp. 3–76. See also Hans Gerth and C. Wright Mills, *Character and Social Structure* (London: Routledge and Kegan Paul, 1954), p. 310: "Classes are anchored, by source and amount of wealth, to the property institutions and occupational roles of the economic order." Moreover, Polanyi argues, classes cannot be understood apart from society as a whole. Indeed, the doctrine of the economic nature of class interests is one-sided at best:

"Though human society is naturally conditioned by economic factors, the

Class Characteristics of Founders and Settlers

Because most of its objective characteristics (property, income, skill) are readily identifiable, class is a convenient point of departure for the analysis of generational change.

The Founders[T] of Germania began their new lives in company with Settlers[N-T] of less education, training, and wealth.[6] Moreover, those who arrived in the fast-growing Turner community later did not share the Founders'[T] sense of mission. Especially was this true for those who settled in Germania after the townspeople had rebuilt their community, all but destroyed by the Sioux Indians in 1862.

Arriving early in Germania, the Turners pre-empted the top positions in the young community. Their desire to transform the wilderness into a socialistic haven was soon modified by opportunities for individual success, and their intention of preserving their traditional ways was short-circuited by plentiful opportunities for wealth, power, and prestige. As Germania grew and prospered, and as it was inundated by non-Turners with money, ability, and ambition, the Turners' class advantage narrowed. The class difference between second-generation Turners and non-Turners was less than that between the first generations. Sons of non-Turners began to match, in education and employment, the positions hitherto inherited or won by sons of Turners. Indeed, the new rise of a competing status elite in Germania, in part composed of middle-man-

motives of human individuals are only exceptionally determined by the needs of material want-satisfaction.

"Purely economic matters such as affect want-satisfaction are incomparably less relevant to class behavior than questions of social recognition. . . . the interests of a class most directly refer to standing and rank, to status and security, that is, they are primarily not economic but social."

Cf. Karl Polanyi, *The Great Transformation* (New York: Rinehart, 1944), p. 153. Finally, Arthur J. Vidich and Joseph Bensman, *Small Town in Mass Society* (Princeton: Princeton University Press, 1958), pp. 78–79, suggest that the basic trend in the American mass economy is "a shift from production to consumption values" by the majority of middle-class employees. As a result, "social class" will eventually replace "economic class" as a meaningful concept. It is hence more realistic to interpret class in social than in economic terms. In this book, however, class is seen as a function of wealth whereas status remains linked to the sources and uses of wealth, regardless of how class in American society may be changing.

[6] See pp. 19–20 for explanation of the terms "Founder[T]," "Settler[N-T]," "Member[T]," and "Non-Member[N-T]."

agement employees of recently arrived regional and national firms —
Kraft Foods, for example — today presents a challenge to the old
Turner elite.

Aspects of Class

Age. Among the many factors associated with the class differences between Turners and non-Turners, age is fundamental. If
large mean differences in age exist between the generational samples,
then one should expect that to some extent age would account for
class differences. For example, non-Turners might have less education and less wealth because they are younger than the Turners.
But the evidence suggests that age is not a factor.[7]

Education. Turners, both husbands and wives, are better educated than non-Turners. Generational comparisons in Table 2 show

Table 2. Generational Comparison of Average Numbers of
Years of Education

	Founder[T]	Member[T]	Settler[N-T]	Non-Member[N-T]
Husband ..	11.3	12.7	9.2	11.3
Wife	11.2	11.8	8.7	8.5

that Members[T] are best educated, Settlers[N-T] least, with Founders[T]
in second place, and Non-Members[N-T] third. Non-Member[N-T] husbands have on the average two years more education than their
fathers. The Turner versus non-Turner educational trend suggests
that the latter may one day reach the Turners' present level of education, but at present the Turners remain superior to the non-
Turners.

Occupational Mobility. The Turner versus non-Turner occupational trend is influenced in part by mobility. As Germania's population has grown, Turnverein membership has dropped since the
turn of the century. Today well-educated sons of Turners do not
ordinarily seek jobs in Germania, even though it has been enlarging
its market of skilled jobs since World War II. Opportunities for
professional careers are limited in Germania, which is already well
supplied with physicians, lawyers, teachers, and the like, whereas

[7] For a comparison of mean ages, see Appendix Table 1.

78

the demand for skilled and semi-skilled workers is rising. (Unskilled and skilled Non-Members [N-T], best fitted to meet this demand, outnumber the proportion of unskilled and skilled Members [T] almost five to one.) Moreover, there are no Turners moving into Germania; they founded the community and stayed, maintaining their group by marriage. Once their sons and daughters marry away from home or move away for other reasons, the possibility of replacement is usually gone.

In both comparative and absolute terms the Turners have a disproportionate amount of Germania's wealth (though much of it is invested outside the community); they hold comparatively more proprietorial and professional positions than non-Turners. Before these comparisons are illustrated, the discussion can be broadened by tracing the main occupational drift of Turners and non-Turners, from grandfathers to grandsons.

Proportionately more fathers of both generations of Turners have held choice occupational positions in the community and elsewhere. Fewer fathers of non-Turner men and women have done as well. More fathers of the first-generation Turners and non-Turners have held less important and remunerative jobs, by today's standards, than their children and grandchildren do. From grandfathers to grandsons there has been a decrease in the proportion of unskilled workers in all groups, but for each generation the proportion of unskilled non-Turner men has been at least twice that of unskilled Turner men. However, this three-generational contrast is not so great for the wives and their fathers. These trends are shown in Table 3.

More fathers of the Founders'[T] wives were proprietors or professionals than those of the Settlers'[N-T] — 28 and 18 per cent respectively. Over twice as many Founders'[T] as Settlers'[N-T] wives are or were before marriage proprietors or professional people. (Most professional people in both groups were nurses or teachers.) The situation is reversed for second-generation wives: 6 per cent of the Members[T] and 16 per cent of the Non-Members[N-T] are married to women in this top occupational category.[8]

[8] See Appendix Table 2.

Husband-Wife Occupational Trends. Though fewer wives of Members [T], as compared with Non-Members [N-T], have ever been fully employed, twice as many of the former (13.5 per cent) have found employment in the clerical and sales field. They have had on the average over three more years of education than the

Table 3. Three-Generation Unskilled
Occupational Trends*

| | Turner | | Non-Turner | |
Generation	Husband	Wife	Husband	Wife
Grandfather	32%	40%	60%	51%
Father	8	68	22	73
Son	6	62	24	54

*Comparisons are of percentages engaged in unskilled occupations. The majority of wives in the unskilled occupational category do not hold jobs (housewives are classified as unskilled), though the proportion of unskilled working wives has increased since the grandfathers' generation.

Non-Members [N-T], and consequently have more easily filled clerical jobs. A first-to-second-generation rise of non-Turner proprietors and professional persons has taken place only among the wives, who have shown an increase of 9 per cent, as compared with a slight decrease (from 29 to 27 per cent) for their husbands. For Turner wives the trend has been the other way around, a 12 per cent decrease (18 to 6) in the proportion of first and second generation proprietors and professionals. The number of Turner husbands in this occupational category has also dropped, from 50 to 35 per cent, Founders [T] to Members [T]. These trends are shown below.

Founders [T], 18%
Members [T], 6%
Settlers [N-T], 7%
Non-Members [N-T], 16%

The occupational advantage secured by the fathers of Founders [T] over the fathers of Settlers [N-T] (half as many of the former unskilled, nearly five times as many proprietors or professionals) has endured to the present day.[9] Turners continue to lead non-Turners in occupations, though their lead has diminished. Yet the second-generation (Members [T] and Non-Members [N-T]) trend appears to show a reassertion of the Turners' long-time occupational superiority. These comparisons and trends are summarized in Tables 4 and 5.

Table 4. First-Generation Occupational Comparisons

Occupational Category	Founders [T]	Settlers [N-T]
Proprietor and professional	50%	29%
Managerial and semiprofessional	16	13
Skilled and unskilled	18	40
Clerical and sales	8	7
Other*	8	11
Total	100%	100%

*Includes retired, deceased, and "No Information." Of the 4 Founders [T] in this classification (8 per cent), 2 (an attorney and a proprietor) are retired, 2 deceased, and 4 could not be placed. Of the six Settlers [N-T], 2 gave no information, 1 is on relief, 1 retired (from a janitorial job), and 2 (formerly an electrician and a painter) are deceased.

Table 5. Second-Generation Occupational Comparisons

Occupational Category	Member [T]	Non-Member [N-T]
Proprietor and professional	35%	27%
Managerial and semiprofessional.	30	11
Skilled and unskilled	12	57
Clerical and sales	18	3
Other*	5	2
Total	100%	100%

*Includes students and "No information."

The proportion of proprietors and professionals in each generation has shifted. Though the Turners continue to show a larger proportion in both occupational classes, their second-generation trend is clearly toward managerial and sales fields. The Turner clerical and sales class (sales predominating) more than doubled in the past generation, and its managerial class increased by almost 100 per cent. The Non-Members [N-T] have actually decreased in both occupational

[9] An occupational comparison of the grandfathers is presented in Appendix Table 3.

classes, and increased by 17 per cent in the skilled and unskilled class. These comparisons do not reveal the generational shift in the proportion of proprietors and professionals. Though the first generation has 8 per cent more Turner than non-Turner professionals, the second generation shows the reverse: 5 per cent more non-Turner than Turner professionals.

	$Founder^T$	$Member^T$	$Settler^{N-T}$	Non-$Member^{N-T}$
Proprietor	40%	29%	27%	16%
Professional	10%	6%	2%	11%

The contrasting occupational preferences of second generation Turners and non-Turners underline their different class backgrounds. A fifth more Members ^{T} than Non-Members $^{N-T}$ prefer to own and manage a small company; almost twice as many of Non-Members as Members chose to occupy, mainly for its greater "security," a middle-management position in a large firm. First generation comparisons, between Founders ^{T} and Settlers $^{N-T}$, are not possible, because a third of the Settlers $^{N-T}$ registered "no response" to this issue. Yet when asked to choose between two "ideal" occupational careers, one a public office and the other in a private firm, well over seven out of ten of all the respondents chose the latter, whereas about one out of ten refused to answer. Most know that the financial rewards of holding office in Germania are meager. Most are petty capitalists at heart, receptive to the virtues of self-employment extolled by their chamber of commerce. Few recognize, it seems, that they are out of step with the main trend in American capitalism as signified by the decline of the independent entrepreneur, who has become rare in Germania as he has elsewhere.

The richer Turners own more property — in automobiles, houses, farms, stores, warehouses, or in business firms — than the non-Turners. The average number of cars owned by Turner families, first and second generation, is 1.6 and 1.7 respectively. Non-Turners own fewer automobiles, both generations averaging about 1.4. Nearly three times as many Founders ^{T} as Settlers $^{N-T}$ own three cars or more, while the ratio of their sons (Member ^{T} versus Non-Member $^{N-T}$) is over 2 to 1. Fewer young than old families, Turner and non-Turner, do not own cars, though Settlers $^{N-T}$ are over four times as likely not to own an automobile as anyone else. Turners also drive later-model automobiles than non-Turners — almost twice as many Founders ^{T} as Settlers $^{N-T}$, 9 per cent more Members ^{T} than Non-Members $^{N-T}$, owned 1960 to 1962 models in 1962. Some of the wealthy Turners drive cars several years old; one, sensitive to his religious minority status in Germania, owned two, one a 1956 and the other a 1957 model, when he could easily afford a new Cadillac every year. "I have to live in this town," he explained. Another, of pioneer stock and one of the most esteemed men of Germania, was content with his 1960 Dodge and his 1956 Oldsmobile. A third, through marriage one of the town's richest citizens, kept a nine-year-old Buick for everyday transportation in addition to two late models.[10]

Ownership of substantial properties — houses, businesses, and the like — is of course more indicative of class standing than possession of automobiles; 22 and 38 per cent of the Turners, 13 and 5 per cent of the non-Turners (first–second generation comparisons in both cases) claim investment in one or more business firms (few own all or even part of more than one firm).[11] Investment in stores, shops, or warehouses, by the same comparison, is held by 26 and 15 per cent of the Turners, 11 and 8 per cent of the non-Turners. Ownership of apartments is, similarly, 16 and 9 per cent (Turners), 4 and 3 per cent (non-Turners). Proportionately fewer of the second than the first generation, and fewer non-Turners than Turners, own property. In percentages, Founders ^{T} own from two to four times more units of property of the kinds mentioned than Settlers $^{N-T}$,

[10] Turners, incidentally, drive more miles per year than non-Turners. Though the proportion of salesmen among Founders and Settlers is about the same, 10 per cent of the Founders drive over 40,000 miles a year, as compared with about 2 per cent of the Settlers. This difference is less between Members and Non-Members, though nearly double the proportion of Members (9 per cent) drive so extensively.

[11] Business firms, or companies, are kept separate here from shops and stores. Examples at random of firms owned by Turners and non-Turners are a brewery, a monument company, the City Salvage Company; construction and trucking companies; a nursery, a lumber company, a floor-covering company, a bus service, and a heating and manufacturing company. There are over two dozen more, too numerous to list — 51 of the 176 respondents are proprietors.

Members[T] two to seven times more than Non-Members[N-T]. These comparisons are not conclusive, however, for the value of the Turners' property may be less than that of the non-Turners'.

In all groups, 70 to 80 per cent own their homes. Though more of the second than the first generation rent, or do not own a house (Members: 18 per cent; Non-Members: 24 per cent), and though about as many Founders[T] (10 per cent) as Settlers[N-T] (13 per cent) rent, Turners live in more expensive houses than non-Turners.[12] Only 4 per cent of the Founders[T] own houses valued at less than $10,000 (averaging $9,000); slightly more than a fourth of the Settlers'[N-T] houses fall in this price category, averaging about $7,350. For Members[T] and Non-Members[N-T] the results are quite different: only one Member[T] and two Non-Members[N-T] own houses in this price class, though one of the Non-Members[N-T] lives in a trailer house ($1,250), the other in a $7,500 house.

At the other price extreme ($30,000 and above), there are more Turners than non-Turners: comparing the percentage of each of

Table 6. Comparison of Turner versus Non-Turner Average Worth and Income

	Founder[T]	Member[T]	Settler[N-T]	Non-Member[N-T]
Value of house	$20,313	$19,732	$15,087	$16,740
Joint income (1962) ..	10,440	8,641	6,416	7,051
Capital investment	58,178*	22,000	21,480	5,875

*One family is worth about $7,000,000 through inheritance (in the form of a trust fund that cannot be drawn upon until the grandchildren reach 21). Only the amount held by the Founder[T] ($750,000) has been included in the computation of the average. If the entire $7,000,000 were included, the average would be $180,725.

the four groups in this price bracket: Founders[T], 16 per cent (averaging over $34,000 per house); Members[T], 9 per cent (over $36,500); Settlers[N-T], not quite 6 per cent ($36,300); and Non-Members[N-T] 0 per cent. The average values of the houses owned by each group are compared, with average incomes and estimates of capital worth, in Table 6. A final comparison of property ownership — in this case the lack thereof — reveals that about 12 per cent of

[12] Of those few who rent, Turners pay an average of $55 to $60 a month, and non-Turners $47 to $70, the second generation paying the higher rent.

each Turner generation (7 and 27 per cent of the first and second non-Turner generations) own no substantial property aside from their homes.

Income and Net Worth. The greatest income and capital worth differences appear among members of the first generation. Founders'[T] incomes range from the man who made only $1,000 in 1962 (a descendant of the founder of Germania, incidentally), to three who made at least $30,000 each. Incomes of Members[T], on the other hand, range from $4,000 to $20,000, one family at each extreme. Settlers[N-T] start and finish lower than Founders[T] from no income (three families) to one with $25,000. Non-Members[N-T] show the narrowest range of all, two at $3,500 and one at $13,500.

The capital worth range has a similar pattern. Considering those who have capital investments, and excluding the $7,000,000 fortune of one Founder, this group's capital worth range begins at about $5,000, of whom there are five, and reaches a peak at something over $750,000 (the personal holdings of the multimillionaire by marriage), followed by two whose holdings approach $250,000 each, and three worth approximately $200,000 apiece. Members[T] can claim no one in the $100,000 class. Their investments range from $5,000 (three) to one who controls $89,000, considerably more than his two closest contenders in the $60,000 bracket. Again, the Settlers[N-T] start lower and end lower than the Founders[T] — one has $3,000 invested, another $400,000. Except for a third with $200,000, the rest have assets of $75,000, $50,000, $25,000, and less. Non-Members[N-T] have not done nearly so well as anyone else. They start high, but end low: $68,000 to $7,500.

The percentage who claim capital investments, or are known to have capital wealth, is considerably higher among Turners than non-Turners. The comparative percentages of all investors are Founders[T] 67 per cent, Settlers[N-T] 35 per cent; Members[T] 62 per cent, Non-Members[N-T] 24 per cent.[13]

The evidence of the Turners' class superiority in Germania is

[13] See Appendix Table 4 for a full comparison of investors and non-investors.

impressive. (See Appendix Table 1 for an account of how these averages were obtained.) All the evidence presented thus far may now be summarized in a final comparison of Germania's wealthy families.

There are approximately fifty families in Germania worth $100,000 or more. Most of them are merchants: Germania's wealthiest businessman, of an old family, made his money in the hardware trade. Another, perhaps twice as rich, is worth about $1,000,000, accumulated from a $50,000–$60,000 a year medical practice and invested in rental property — a bank and two or three retail stores on Germania's main business street. A third operates a women's clothing store in Germania and owns several large apartment buildings in Minneapolis. A hardware dealer, a physician, a clothier — these are Germania's wealthiest three. The second is a Turner; these three do not include the multimillionaire, also a Turner, whose wealth is largely potential.

Others are less wealthy: one merchant responded to a friend's request for a business loan by writing a personal check for $40,000, casually forgoing making a written record of the transaction. The widow of another found, when opening her husband's safe deposit box in the presence of probate examiners, an unexpected fortune of $197,000 in currency. There is wealth in Germania. Much of it was made in land and stock speculation. Most of it has accumulated steadily for the past three generations from carefully managed merchant-trading ventures. Only a small part is derived from manufacturing, which since World War II has for the first time emerged as a major new source of wealth.

Of the fifty families in Germania worth $100,000 or more, twenty-five were selected on the basis of their capital holdings. Knowledge about these holdings was gained either by asking the men themselves for estimates or, when this was not feasible, by asking others thoroughly familiar with the men to make estimates. The informants included a manufacturer, a corporation lawyer, and a retired merchant, all of whom have lived in Germania for at least twenty years. A list of the twenty-five wealthiest families, including every Turner family in the $100,000 bracket (and a few who were not interviewed) was compiled, separated into Turners and non-Turners, totaled, and divided by the number of families in each group. (None of the other twenty-five rich families has more extensive holdings than the holdings of those selected.) The interesting results are shown in Table 7.

Since there were in 1962 only a hundred and twenty-one resident Turner families among Germania's population of twelve thousand,

Table 7. Total Mean Capital Worth of Germania's 25
Wealthiest Families *

	Turner (N = 10)	Non-Turner (N = 15)
Total capital worth	$3,150,000	$3,800,000
Mean capital worth	315,000†	160,000

*Only one has made its money in manufacturing; the others are merchants, physicians, and attorneys.

†If, as in Table 6, the potential wealth of the multimillionaire Founder [T] is included in the calculation, the mean capital worth of the Turners becomes $940,000.

and 40 per cent of the community's twenty-five richest families are Turners, there can be little doubt that they are an upper status group of considerable wealth.

Most of the money remains in the hands of the property owners, but irregular lines of skirmish are being formed by the new occupational elite — young attorneys, managers, insurance agents, dentists, and physicians, who challenge the old line, heavy with property. Still, in Germania today the wealthy are men of property. Turners own proportionately more property than non-Turners do. Turners earn more than non-Turners do, and they have comparatively more money.

Scale Comparisons of Class

The findings about the relative class standing of Turners and non-Turners have, in every way examined, supported the main hypothesis of this chapter: Turners occupy class positions superior to those held by non-Turners. In addition, the evidence for the second generation has shown that in some, but not all, instances Non-Members [N-T] are moving toward a station in life comparable with that

87

enjoyed by Members [T] and higher than that achieved by Germania's Settlers [N-T]. Turners continue to hold their own, but the gap between them and non-Turners is closing.

The class scale, if sensitive, should afford a statistical verification of the descriptive findings. It will be recalled that each of the thirteen items on the class scale may be responded to in scores ranging from

Table 8. Generational Comparison of Class, Divided into 3 Groups *

Scale Category	Founder[T]		Member[T]		Settler[N-T]		Non-Member[N-T]	
	No.	%	No.	%	No.	%	No.	%
High (39–52)	17	41.4	12	46.1	7	16.8	5	15.6
Medium (25–38) ..	19	46.3	12	46.1	18	42.8	21	65.6
Low (11–24)	5	12.3	2	7.7	17	40.4	6	18.8
Total	41	100.0	26	99.9	42	100.0	32	100.0

*χ^2, Founder[T] vs. Settler[N-T], $= 10.7$, 2 d.f., $p<.01$.

one to five, signifying lowest to highest class standing.[14] Since the scale is ordinal, it does not assume equal intervals from one to five; also, since the items are varied, it cannot be assumed that a score of, say, three has the same value or meaning for one item of the class scale as for any other. Consequently, a comparison of the mean scale scores of the four generational subsamples would be meaningless. Computation of the scale data is therefore straightforward, achieved by totaling the class score of each family and then counting the frequencies of high, medium, and low scores in each group.

My theory predicts that Founders [T] occupy a class position higher than Settlers [N-T], Members [T] higher than Non-Members [N-T]; though the second-generation distance is less than the first. Two adjustments were made to allow the comparison of group scale scores. (Obviously each family must answer all items when mean scores are not computed.) First, items twelve and thirteen, not answered by 14 to 36 per cent of the respondents, were omitted in order to retain statistically comparable samples. Second, those respondents who did not answer all eleven of the remaining scale items were dropped, result-

[14] See the class scale, pp. 162–164, Appendix 2.

ing in adjusted samples containing 41, 26, 42, and 32 — first-generation Turners, second-generation Turners, first-generation non-Turners, and second-generation non-Turners.[15]

Class scale scores were divided into three groups: high (39–52), medium (25–38), and low (11–24), representing the actual range of scores, 12–51, achieved by the 141 respondents. Generational

Table 9. Generational Comparison of Class, Divided into 2 Groups *

Scale Category	Founder[T] No.	%	Member[T] No.	%	Settler[N-T] No.	%	Non-Member[N-T] No.	%
High (32–51)	28	68.3	18	69.2	17	40.5	11	34.5
Low (12–31)	13	31.7	8	30.8	25	59.5	21	65.5
Total	41	100.0	26	100.0	42	100.0	32	100.0

*χ^2, Founder[T] vs. Member[T], $= 0.12$, 1 d.f., not significant. χ^2, Settler[N-T] vs. Non-Member[N-T], $= .09$, 1 d.f., not significant.

and Turner versus non-Turner comparisons were made of the frequency of scores in each of the three categories. These comparisons are summarized in Tables 8 and 9.

To test the significance of differences between the generations, the scale scores were regrouped into two categories: high (32–51) and low (12–31). Regrouped generational comparisons of scores may be tested for significance as shown in Table 9. Generational differences within each group (e.g., Founder versus Member) are, as expected, not significant. It is apparent that second-generation Turners (Members) occupy a higher class position than their non-Turner age-mates (Non-Members). The class advantage of the former is considerable, but it is not so rare, statistically, as the Founder[T] versus Settler[N-T] difference: the probability that Members[T] are in a higher class than Non-Members[N-T] is more than ninety-eight times out of a hundred; that Founders[T] outrank

[15] See pp. 19–20 for a discussion of these four samples. Conceivably, the rejection of several cases from each sample may have biased the results. Turners may only seem to show more high scores than non-Turners. All rejected cases were inspected and compared; their exclusion seems not to have altered the findings significantly. See pp. 153, 156, Appendix 1 for an extensive analysis of the rejected cases.

Settlers[N-T] more than ninety-nine times out of a hundred.[16] In both cases the differences are not due to chance.

Finally, an over-all Turner versus non-Turner comparison was made as shown in Table 10. Turners lead non-Turners by a wide margin in access to local and non-local economic opportunities.

Conclusion

Descriptive and scale data offer conclusive proof that first and second generations of Germania's Turners form a local class elite. The trend, however, is unmistakable: Non-Members[N-T] (or second-generation non-Turners) are catching up; their bid for a proportionately larger share of Germania's wealth has been demonstrated.

Not all Turners have done exceptionally well in Germania. Some have risen from humble origins and become wealthy. Others ac-

Table 10. Turner versus Non-Turner Comparison of Class *

Scale Category	Turner		Non-Turner	
	No.	%	No.	%
High (39–52)	29	43.3	12	16.2
Medium (25–38)	31	46.3	39	52.7
Low (11–24)	7	10.4	23	31.1
Total	67	100.0	74	100.0

$*\chi^2$, Turner vs. non-Turner, $= 16.3, 2$ d.f., $p<.001$.

cumulated considerable wealth in the course of their lives only to have it dissipated by their heirs. A few failed to make any financial progress. Of those who, in the eyes of the community, were successful, some achieved material success by hard work and business acumen; some gambled in stocks or land; some married into rich families; and a few entered one or another of the professions and carved out brilliant careers for themselves.

[16] A test of the difference between Members[T] and Non-Members[N-T] (Table 9) yielded a chi square of 5.6, significant with one degree of freedom at $<.02$, as compared with a Founder[T] versus Settler[N-T] chi square (Table 8) of 10.7, significant at $<.01$.

¶ chapter 5

STATUS DISTINCTION AND ETHNIC AMALGAMATION

CONSOLIDATING their prestige in Germania, forming an honorific in-group, the Turners abandoned Turnerism. Thus the link between ethnicity and status was, for Germania's Turners, inverse and causal: prestige in the wider community was won at the expense of their Old World heritage. Whatever might be said about the outcome, the decision of the Turners to transfer their entire loyalty to America was a matter of deliberate policy. Turnerism was identified with Americanism as early as 1872, when the National Executive Committee of the American Gymnastic Union announced its disassociation from German Turnerism.[1] Earlier, in 1853, the American Turnvereine had resolved to establish schools, the main purpose of which was to initiate German immigrants into American practices, "to inculcate in them American ideals," and to teach them the

---

[1] Weier, *op. cit.*, pp. 10–13. Turners served their adopted land with devotion: "Over 75% of all Turners in the United States were in active service" during the Civil War, observes Weier. To become a member of a Turnverein one has to be a citizen of the United States or declare one's intention of becoming a citizen — a rule strictly enforced by every American Turnverein since 1848. Turners quickly identified themselves with national interests, teaching the American constitution and history in the night and Sunday schools maintained by Turner societies throughout the United States and making "political demands" of the nation well before any other organizations took them up — such demands as the secret ballot, the direct election of senators by the people, and proportional representation. In short, American Turnvereine "acted as Americanization agencies."

language.[2] If anything, the Germania Turners excelled in the American Turner practice of accommodating themselves to the habits and values of their new fatherland as expeditiously as possible. In Germania as across the nation, Turnerism consciously inaugurated a policy that would accelerate the decline of its Old World ethnicity.

Assimilation

The journey of the Turners from Europe to North America and their transformation from an ethnic to a status community undeniably brought them to new thresholds of experience and gave them new habits of mind. These major dislocations, in which an old way of life is gradually buried under culturally and socially dominant forms, are expressed by the concept of assimilation.[3] To the extent,

[2] Kuecken, *op. cit.*, p. 7.

[3] Though many American sociologists use the terms "assimilation" and "acculturation" interchangeably, the former is preferred here because of the special meaning anthropologists attach to the latter. American anthropologists have generally regarded acculturation as a kind of culture change in which one culture is considerably altered in conformity to another culture but does not in the process lose its separate identity. Culture contact is seen as the precipitating vehicle of acculturation, a process which inevitably leads to modifications in both cultures. Assimilation, on the other hand, is commonly regarded by anthropologists as a completed affair, the last stage of acculturation, whereas sociologists speak of phases of assimilation, arguing that second-generation American immigrants typically represent a transitional phase, third-generation immigrants an all but final phase. Moreover, anthropologists emphasize the alterations of whole cultures and the emergence of new cultural patterns in the acculturation process whereas sociologists stress the changes in group behavior, the modifications of institutions, and the inculcation of new goals and values in those being assimilated. The differences are more than terminological; they reflect quite different theoretical perspectives, especially as to how students of each discipline conceptualize the relation between culture, society, and social organization. In view of these differences, the concept of assimilation is used in this book, and it will be regarded as denoting a largely one-way process, partly forced and partly voluntary, by which the members of an alien guest community or group adapt themselves to the way of life of a host community, successive generations of aliens giving up more and more of their native culture until they are virtually undistinguishable from their hosts. See Milton M. Gordon, *Assimilation in American Life* (New York: Oxford University Press, 1964), pp. 60–83, for a discussion of stages of assimilation; Ralph Beals, "Acculturation," in A. L. Kroeber, ed., *Anthropology Today* (Chicago: University of Chicago Press, 1953), pp. 621–641, for a review of the history of the concept of acculturation in American anthropology and its ambiguities; Sirjamaki, *op. cit.*, pp. 225–231; W. Lloyd Warner, *American Life: Dream and Reality*, (Chicago: University of Chicago Press, rev. ed., 1962), pp. 179–197; and for a recent discussion of the

therefore, that the Turners have become a status community in Germania, one would expect them to have abandoned their old cultural identity, their minority psychology, and their former goals and values, and to have assumed the mental and behavioral attitudes of North Americans. They have become Americans.

In this book the process of assimilation is examined in two main aspects: the changes in the Old World ethnicity of the Turners as Germans, and the changes in their ideological suppositions as

Table 11. Percentage of Husbands and Wives
of German Parentage *

	Turner		Non-Turner	
Generation	Husband	Wife	Husband	Wife
First	86%	66%	71%	71%
Second	71%	50%	54%	49%

*The complete German versus non-German ethnic composition of all groups is presented in Appendix Table 8.

Turners. Both their ethnic and their ideological alienness marked the immigrant Turners of Germania for initial closure into a minority community. Their emergence as a status community required considerable modification of their German cultural heritage to conform to the tenets of Americans. By the same token, their ideological and political inheritance as Turners, in which they sought the realization of their Old World nationalist aspirations through partly collectivist, partly individualist programs for reform and utopian schemes, was incongruous in Germania, the more so as they assumed status community form.

The Blend of Ethnicity

As may be seen in Table 11, Turners are somewhat more German in origin than non-Turners, though the proportion of husbands and wives of German background has decreased in the second genera-

practical implications of finding that acculturation exhibits similar stages under common stimuli in historically unrelated parts of the world, see George M. Foster, *Traditional Cultures: And the Impact of Technological Change* (New York: Harper and Row, 1962), pp. 25–43.

tion. Half to two thirds as many Turners as non-Turners are part German. Similarly, there are more non-Turner than Turner husbands of non-German origin (about double the proportion), whereas from one third as many to two times more Turners (both generations) than non-Turners are married to non-German women, the proportion increasing with the second generation. Proportionately more German Turner men than non-Turner men are married to non-German women, a trend strongest among the second generation, indicating the Turners' relatively pronounced acceptance of the wider community's ways.

One of the surest signs of the eclipse of ethnicity is intermarriage. Turners are more exogamous ethnically, but not residentially, than non-Turners.[4] This apparent contradiction is explained by the fact that of those young Turner men who have remained in Germania (and they are comparatively few), many have married daughters of non-Turners. Turners and non-Turners express equal unconcern about whom their daughters should marry, a German or a non-German. Thus, less than 3 per cent of all groups said that they were most strongly opposed to a "mixed nationality" marriage for their daughters. Racial intermarriage is, of course, least tolerable of all, religious intermarriage next to the least.[5]

Casual observation supports these findings: known to this writer are several recent cases of daughters of prominent old German families marrying, with full parental approval, non-German "outsiders." Turners and non-Turners, several times more in favor of "mixed nationality" marriage than mixed class or status marriage,

[4] Proportionately more male Turners (40 and 32 per cent) have married within Germania than non-Turners (27 and 30 per cent), from first to second generation in both cases. Conversely, about six out of ten Turner wives, seven out of ten non-Turner wives, were born outside Germania. Founders are least exogamous, Settlers most. However, the difference in the wives' residential mobility is not great.

Turner residential mobility has been comparatively slight. A greater proportion of non-Turners than Turners was born outside Germania — from 71 to 65 per cent of first- and second-generation non-Turners — as compared to 46 and 47 per cent of first- and second-generation Turners. Twice as many Founders[T] as Settlers[N-T], and 18 per cent more Members[T] than Non-Members[N-T] were born in Germania. (The names given to these generational units are explained on pp. 19–20.)

[5] See question 103, Appendix 3.

do not differ in this regard. As predicted, Turners do not respond at all like an ethnic minority; they are more conscious of class and status than of nationality.[6] Daughters should not marry below their status. Though from 80 to 90 per cent of all groups believed it did not matter whether their daughters marry men from Germania, three fourths of the respondents held definite opinions about what constitutes a "best marriage." An overwhelming majority replied that a daughter could not do better than to marry an intelligent, industrious young man who loves her. Yet from half to three quarters of each group regarded interfaith marriages, for their daughters, as second in undesirability to racial intermarriage.

Old World Associations

Less than one out of ten of the first generation, husband or wife, were born in Europe. Though no second-generation respondents were born in Europe, Members[T] have more immediate Old World origins than Non-Members[N-T]; grandfathers of half of the Members[T], as compared with a third of the Non-Members[N-T], emigrated to North America. Almost equal proportions of the fathers of all respondents (husbands and wives) were born in Europe: about a fourth to a third of the fathers of Founders[T] and Settlers[N-T], and 6 to 12 per cent of the fathers of Members[T] and Non-Members[N-T]. In all groups fewer wives than husbands had fathers who were foreign-born.

Comparisons of their associations with Europe, and particularly with Germany, reveal one distinct pattern of differences between Turners and non-Turners: Founders[T] maintain closest ties with Germany, followed by Members.[T] Settlers[N-T] and Non-Members[N-T], in that order, have looser ties with people in the old country.

Despite more contacts with Germany, Turners have formed fewer personal associations with its people than have non-Turners: about two fifths of the Founders[T] and three fifths of the Members[T] do not know anyone living in Germany. All Non-Members[N-T] have

[6] For example, though only 8 to 21 per cent of the respondents "most preferred" mixed status marriages, and from 4 to 11 per cent "most preferred" mixed class marriages, five to six out of every ten showed the greatest preference for (or least objection to) marriages of mixed nationality.

acquaintances and relatives there, whereas less than 2 per cent of the Settlers [N-T] know no one in Germany. Fully 70 per cent of the non-Turners and less than 10 per cent of the Turners know at least one person in Germany. On the other hand, some Founders [T] claim ten or twelve acquaintances, friends, and relatives in Germany — one, a German-born veterinarian in his sixties, said he knew five hundred people in the fatherland. (Only two others in the entire study — a Founder [T] and a Settler [N-T], both first generation — knew an unusually large number of Old World Germans, but even so, far fewer than claimed by the veterinarian: twenty-five each.) Fewer Settlers [N-T] than Founders [T] have more than five personal acquaintances in Germany, whereas not one Non-Member [N-T] or Member [T] knows as many as ten German citizens.[7] While, in addition, proportionately more Founders [T] than Settlers [N-T] have good friends or relatives in Germany (42 and 26 per cent, respectively) — the second generation showing little difference in this regard — this comparison is not to imply that the Founders [T] know more people in Germany. Half of the Founders [T] and almost all of the Settlers [N-T] know from one to more than three persons in Germany. In short, non-Turners know more Germans in Germany, whereas Founders [T] alone know them better.

Ethnicity may also be described in terms of the number of "outsiders" (non-Germans) that descendants of immigrants know. Though more than eight out of ten male Founders [T] are of German descent, as compared with seven out of ten male Settlers [N-T], there is no difference in the relative number of good friends of non-German origin claimed by each. Though slightly fewer Founders [T] (14 per cent) than Settlers [N-T] (18 per cent) have no non-German friends, more of the latter (almost two thirds) than the former (just over half) have as many as six friends who are not Germans. (A few men in each group said they had twenty-five, fifty, or "a great many" non-German friends.) The second generation, who are themselves less German, have more non-German friends: less than one out of ten has no non-German friends; roughly seven out of ten

[7] Complete comparisons of the number of persons known in Germany are given in Appendix Table 9.

have six or more. Again, there is very little difference between the groups.[8]

Despite sporadic attempts such as the following to repair them, Germania's links with the Old World have been shattered. In 1962 the community celebrated the hundredth anniversary of the Sioux uprising of 1862. Throughout the week-long series of events — mock battles, re-enactment of the flight of the townsmen and the arrival of the troops, parades, public ceremonies, and speeches — Germania's history was recalled and extolled. To the stranger, Germania's origins were apparent. To this observer, nothing in that commemorative week was so interesting as the duality, or perhaps one should say the ambiguity, of Germania's part in American history. During that week Germania recalled two histories — pioneer American and immigrant German. The main event of the week, a two-hour parade, dramatized both histories; interspersed among the usual floats advertising local industry and associations were troupes of stereotyped Indians, pioneer wagons driven by "early settlers," old-time German bands, German-costumed "immigrants," Bavarian beer wagons, and antique American vehicles. The parade passed by Turner Hall, where earlier that day townspeople had met and talked with Dr. Theodor Pfizer, burgomaster of a prominent West German city, and Mr. Hans T. Joohs, director of defense of that city, former home of many of Germania's first settlers.

Germania's city fathers had invited the burgomaster and his associate in honor of the occasion. The Turnverein received them with German music, feted them with German food and locally brewed German beer which flowed from barrels in the Bier Garten especially constructed in Turner Park and was served by waiters in German costume. During the reception a conversation between a local editor, a member of Germania's city council, and Dr. Pfizer led to a comparison of German and American traditions. The general tone of their remarks conveyed mild regret over the decline of old German customs, both in America and in Germany — tele-

[8] Members[T] seem to have more non-German friends than Non-Members[N-T]. However, four times as many of the latter (13 per cent) did not answer, or replied ambiguously, to the question, "How many friends do you have who are not of German origin?"

vision, for example, was compared unfavorably with live theater. Dr. Pfizer remarked: "Television, to me, in comparison to being right there [in the theater], is the difference between homemade soup and canned soup." All agreed wholeheartedly. The discussion drifted on to the subject of the dance. One Turner, a young college teacher, assured the burgomaster that Germania observes some old-country traditions with more authenticity than Germany itself; the twist, then popular in Germany, was his example, which he maintained no one in Germania dances. "We prefer the old-time polka," he said. (Germania advertises itself as the Polka Capital of the nation; it claims over a dozen "old-time" bands.) Everyone voiced concern over the steady rise of "alien" ways in Germania; they agreed that forty or fifty years ago Germania was a distinctively German town. ("The manuscript census of 1860 reveals that only one family and one single man of American name and descent resided in the city." All other families of New Ulm were at least part German. "New Ulm was practically a German city."[9]) Several informants then confided to this writer that there are few "real Turners" in Germania today, claiming that the town has lost its Old World character. Though the *New Ulm Daily Journal* editorializes on the town's *Gemütlichkeit*, no one really believes this sentiment; while the local cinema advertised, in bad German, "The Bridge — *Deutsch De Sprechen*,"[10] few of its patrons read German books or newspapers.

Turners and non-Turners alike have fully embraced the American way of life, for "The making of an American begins at that point where he himself rejects all other ties, any other history, and himself adopts the vesture of his adopted land. This problem has been faced by all Americans throughout our history — in a way it *is* our history — and it baffles the immigrant and sets on edge the second generation until today."[11] Preference for America is strongest among members of the second generation. They show less interest in Europe, including Germany, than their parents. Not very many

[9] *New Ulm Daily Journal*, June 26, 1962, p. 6.
[10] August 30, 1962.
[11] James Baldwin, *Notes of a Native Son* (Boston: Beacon Press, 1955), p. 29.

Turners or non-Turners would like to see their children educated in Europe: six to seven out of ten definitely would not. About one out of ten of those who would like to see their children educated abroad chose Germany as the best place to study — with the exception of the Members [T], of whom almost one out of five expressed a preference for Germany. Somewhat more Turners, about 12 per cent of each generation, than non-Turners — Settlers [N-T] 9 per cent, and Non-Members [N-T] 3 per cent — did not care where their children received their schooling — Europe or North America.

Further evidence that the second generation more than the first has rejected the homeland of their fathers appears in a comparison of responses to the question: "If you were to move to another country, where would you most prefer to spend the rest of your life?" [12] The first generation showed the clearest preference for Germany, Founders [T] 40 per cent, and Settlers [N-T] 35 per cent; the rest had no preference, or chose Scandinavia, England, France, or Italy, in that order. Interest in living in Germany, however, was not marked among the second generation. Germania's younger generations have acquired a forgetfulness or indifference about their origins which is not fully given to their elders.

Language: The Last Link

Nowhere is this indifference so strongly reflected as in language, which is at the core of the immigrant's sense of ethnicity. [13] The immigrant who adopts the language of his adopted country, allowing his native tongue to slip into disuse, has let go: he is assimilated. [14] Germania's Turners have let go more completely than many of their non-Turner neighbors.

The second generation is considerably less interested than the first in preserving the German language, which they seldom speak and almost never read. First-generation Turners, who also are much

[12] See question 38 of the questionnaire, Appendix 3.

[13] Warner, *op. cit.*, pp. 185–186, remarks: "Language is . . . indispensable to the persistence of a social system . . . those ethnics who speak English will tend to assimilate more rapidly than those who do not."

[14] Simirenko's study, for example, of an ethnic community in transition (*op. cit.*, pp. 168–172) supports this generalization. See also Warner and Srole, *op. cit.*, pp. 220ff.

more comfortable with English, show more interest in German than their sons and daughters do. Loss of concern for the German language among Members[T] and Non-Members[N-T] would be expected on the basis of a single comparison: the proportion of the parents of each generation who spoke only German. Comparing along the male line of descent, 20 per cent of the parents of Founders[T] and 15 per cent of the parents of Settlers[N-T] spoke only German, whereas less than 3 per cent of the Members'[T] and Non-Members'[N-T] parents spoke only German.[15] Conversely, 8 to 16 per cent, respectively, of Founders'[T] and Settlers'[N-T] parents, as compared with 24 and 30 per cent, respectively, of Members'[T] and Non-Members'[N-T] parents knew only English. About an equal proportion of each group's parents spoke German as well as English: roughly three fourths of the Founders'[T] and Members'[T], two thirds of the Settlers'[N-T] and Non-Members'[N-T].

More of the first than of the second generation learned both German and English in childhood. Of those who have spoken both languages since childhood, Founders[T] are most strongly represented (58 per cent, males only), as contrasted to 40 per cent bilingual male Settlers[N-T]. Fewer individuals of the second generation learned German in childhood, and conversely more of them learned English while young, and German some time later. (More non-Turners than Turners, of both generations, learned German as children.) Thus, comparing Turner and non-Turner males, about 10 per cent more Turners of both generations are bilingual, though in all cases the second generation is less so. On the other hand, 10 and 6 per cent of Founders[T] and Members[T], 18 and 16 per cent of Settlers[N-T] and Non-Members[N-T], learned German in their youth. Finally, only 4 per cent of the Founders[T] and 2 per cent of the Settlers[N-T] learned English first, then German, whereas many more Members[T] and Non-Members[N-T] — 27 and 14 per cent in each instance — learned English before learning German. Turners, more exposed to public school education than non-Turners (more of whom attended parochial schools, where instruction in the German language predomi-

[15] The respondents were asked what language was spoken at home during their childhood.

nated for a longer time), have adopted the English language more completely than non-Turners.

Turners show less daily use and interest of German than non-Turners. Hardly anyone in Germania reads German-language newspapers, books, or magazines. The highest proportion of any group who read anything in German is 18 per cent (male Founders [T]); the lowest is less than 2 per cent (male Settlers [N-T]). In only one case, the 3 per cent of the male Members [T] who read German-language books or magazines, does the second generation show any habitual tendency or ability to read literature in German — indeed, their excursions into the language of their forebears are sporadic and uncertain. Wives read German even less than husbands; no wife of a Non-Member [N-T] reads anything in German. The comparison in Table 12 of German-language reading habits is typical.

Table 12. Percentage of Men Who Read German-Language
Books * or Magazines

Response	Founder [T]	Member [T]	Settler [N-T]	Non-Member [N-T]
Do not read	80%	91.2%	87.3%	100%
Do read	18	2.9	7.2	
No response	2	5.9	5.5	

*Including the Bible.

Finally, the vast majority use and prefer to use the English language. First- versus second-generation comparisons of the extent to which only English is spoken in the home are Turners, 82 and 94 per cent; non-Turners, 71 and 100 per cent. Again, Settlers [N-T] speak German more extensively than Founders [T]: though 10 per cent more Founders [T] than Settlers [N-T] prefer the German language above all others (except English), 72 versus 62 per cent, twice as many of the Settlers [N-T] express interest in teaching their children German or having them learn it: Settlers [N-T], 53 per cent, Founders [T], 26 per cent. The second generation, Members [T] and Non-Members [N-T], shows still less concern for German: 62 and 54 per cent, respectively, chose German as the foreign language they most prefer. Furthermore, they are plainly uninterested in having their children learn German; once again, fewer than one out of five says that this would be desirable; more Members[T] (68 per cent) than Non-Members[N-T] (60 per cent) say that it would not. Turners, whose origin is more German than the non-Turners, are the most fully assimilated sector of Germania's population.

Scale Analysis of Assimilation

The Turners' transformation from an ethnic to a status community involved the loss of their original cultural heritage. Descriptively it has been established that the Turners of Germania are ethnically indistinct from their non-Turner neighbors, thus confirming the hypothesis that the Turners are a status and not an ethnic subcommunity. The results of the assimilation scale further support this hypothesis.

According to our predictions, no pronounced Turner versus non-Turner differences in assimilation should exist.[16] What seem to be considerably stronger Germanic identifications among Settlers[N-T] than among Founders[T] — revealed in a marked difference between first- and second-generation non-Turners — are not themselves verified statistically. For purposes of statistical comparison — and employing the logic of scale analysis of Chapter 5 — assimilation scale scores have been divided into two groups — low (9–25) and high (26–41). Table 13 compares the frequency with which Settlers[N-T] and Non-Members[N-T] achieved low or high scores.

Comparisons of the scores made by each group on nine items of the assimilation scale demonstrate that there is no difference be-

[16] Chi square tests of the significance of differences between the groups yielded Turner versus non-Turner, $\chi^2 = 1.23$; Founder[T] versus Settler[N-T], $\chi^2 = 1.32$; Founder[T] versus Member[T], $\chi^2 = 1.88$ — none significant. Adjustments were again made affecting the original assimilation scale and reducing the size of each sample. Scale items 1 and 2 were dropped to preserve statistically feasible sample sizes — from 50 to 68 per cent of the respondents did not respond to these items. Item 12, also excluded from the statistical analysis, does not discriminate appreciably between Turners and non-Turners. From about 9 to 27 per cent of each group, those who did not answer all the remaining nine items, were omitted, reducing the original samples to Founder[T], 38; Member[T], 31; Settler[N-T], 46; and Non-Member[N-T], 36. Analysis of the rejected cases, whose inclusion may conceivably alter the statistical results, indicates that in all likelihood this is not so. P. 153 presents a more complete analysis of the rejected cases.

Table 13. Generational Comparison of Assimilation *

Scale Category	Settler[N-T]		Non-Member[N-T]	
	No.	%	No.	%
High (26–41)	15	32.6	2	5.6
Low (9–25)	31	67.4	34	94.4
Total	46	100.0	36	100.0

*χ^2, Settler[N-T] vs. Non-Member[N-T], $= 7.42$, 1 d.f., $p<.01$. See Appendix 1 for tabular comparisons of the assimilation scale results of all groups.

tween Turners and non-Turners or between Founders[T] and Settlers[N-T], and no difference between first- and second-generation Turners; second-generation non-Turners are significantly more assimilated (or less German) than their fathers' generation, whereas second-generation Turners are statistically identical with second-generation non-Turners.[17]

Despite their vigorous German heritage, and consequent upon their acquisition of prestige in Germania, the Turners have become rather more fully assimilated into the mainstream of American culture than the non-Turners. Some of them regret, at times, the price of status; oldtimers remark that real Turnerism, as they knew it, is not now practiced in Germania. For the first time in the history of Germania's Turnverein a non-Turner of Scandinavian origin was, in 1962, hired as director of physical education. With this unprecedented event the weakened core of the Germania Turner tradition, gymnastics, was reduced to a shadow of its former existence. Those few Turners who fondly recall the Turnverein's proudest days take little part in its present unfamiliar activities.

Status

Status Groups in Germania. Three distinct high-status groupings exist in Germania. Each lays claim to honor and cultivates a style of life partly at odds with but also somewhat indistinguishable from

[17] The probability is less than once in a hundred that Non-Members[N-T] are more assimilated than Settlers[N-T] purely by chance. A 2 x 2 chi square test of Member[T] versus Non-Member[N-T] differences ($\chi^2 = 0.13$) resulted in identical observed and expected frequencies of response in the assimilation scale.

that of the others. These groupings, formed of overlapping strata, may be distinguished on the basis of the age of their wealth. Old, prestigeful wealth is concentrated in the hands of a comparatively few Founders[T] and Settlers[N-T]. Founders[T] comprise the highest status stratum, Settlers[N-T] the next, and some second-generation descendants, joined by newcomers from the second generation, form the third highest stratum. New wealth, in the hands of the rising tide of propertyless managers, salesmen, insurance agents, young professionals, and semiprofessional men, is earned; its claims to prestige rest mainly on education and occupation and, to a lesser extent, on marriage. Members[T] and especially Non-Members[N-T] who do not possess old family wealth therefore form an emergent status group, ranked third, which is beginning to shift the terms of prestige in Germania. On the other hand, the prestige of some Members[T] and Non-Members[N-T] — sons and daughters who inherit old wealth — remains higher; to them falls the task of preserving the prestige of Germania's old families.

Status: General Characteristics. In their pure form, class characteristics are objective. Status properties, by contrast, are subjective; they are manifest as claims to honor and the pursuit of an exclusive, personal style of life.[18] Though the status order controls the consumption of certain goods (which amounts to restrictions on the market),[19] the distinctive feature of status is not property but *honor*. A phenomenon of the social order,[20] the basic categories of status are honor or the lack of honor. Honor may be recognized by any group — even thieves. Honor may become a dominant civilizational theme, as for example its military stylization in the courts and on the plains of medieval knighthood. The rise and fall of an exquisitely refined style of life sustained by great wealth and regulated by a code of honor is a common literary theme, sometimes told with un-

---

[18] Gerth and Mills, *Weber*, p. 192. "If mere economic acquisition and naked economic power still bearing the stigma of its extra-status origin could bestow upon anyone who has won it the same honor as those who are interested in status by virtue of style of life claim for themselves, the status order would be threatened at its very root."

[19] *Ibid.*, pp. 192–193.

[20] *Ibid.*, p. 194. The social order is "the sphere of the distribution of 'honor.'"

common felicity and grace.[21] Though status honor often is enhanced by property and wealth, it need not be. In fact, "it normally stands in sharp opposition to the pretensions of sheer property."[22]

Members of a status group characteristically observe a specific *style of life*,[23] which is intimately linked with their claims to honor. The style of life cultivated by a status group is often restricted against outsiders. Such restrictions placed on members and non-members seek to preserve advantage to the in-group. For example, restrictions are set up on social intercourse with outsiders, usually on marriage, on employment, and even on conventions of dress and speech, reinforcing the qualities of distance and exclusiveness peculiar to the status group.

Objectively, status is manifest in the fact that "every style of life of a status group requires a certain level of consumption."[24] Classes are stratified in their relations to the production and acquisition of goods, whereas status groups are stratified by their consumption of goods; that is, by the material expressions of their special styles of life.[25]

In the present assessment of status the main emphasis is on the behavior that reveals the cultivation of a distinct style of life by an upper status community of Turners. In Germania, honorific or prestigeful qualities are felt to lie in entertaining or pursuing various local and extra-local interests and activities, such as participation in the "cultural" events of the community — concerts and lectures, educational associations, exclusive lawn parties, gala balls, and the like.

Style of Life

The style of life of Germania's Turners has changed radically since the turn of the century. There was a time when the Turners were recognized as the cultural and intellectual leaders of the com-

[21] See, for example, Giuseppe di Lampedusa, *The Leopard*, trans. by Archibald Colquhoun (New York: Pantheon Books, 1960).

[22] Gerth and Mills, *Weber*, p. 187.

[23] *Ibid.*, "In content, status honor is normally expressed by the fact that above all else a specific *style of life* can be expected from all those who wish to belong to the circle."

[24] Martindale, *American Social Structure*, p. 449.

[25] Gerth and Mills, *Weber*, p. 193.

munity; when plays and operas were performed by European artists on the stage of their Turner Hall; when dances, banquets, lectures and concerts, school instruction, public meetings, law sessions, and gymnastic festivals — all held at the Turner Hall — occupied much of their leisure. In January, 1901, the greater part of the community, joined by scores of Turners from Minneapolis and St. Paul, solemnly dedicated the third new Turner Hall. By then, however, the intellectual life of the Turnverein had passed its peak of the 1890's, though a new era of the cultivation of the arts, foreshadowed by the construction of a fine theater in the new Hall, was about to be initiated.[26] Although the Turnverein's most exciting period of cultural activity, from 1900 to 1935, did not survive the Depression,[27] the post-Depression recovery of Germania's cultural life outside Turner Hall put an end to the Turners' historic pre-eminence.

The style of life of contemporary Turners reflects the distance they have traveled since the First World War, a crucial turning point in German-American relations.[28] Though their Turner heritage has faded to the point of being unrecognizable, they have succeeded in establishing a new identity as Americans. Their transformed identity is partly revealed in the following Turner versus non-Turner comparisons of status.

Reading Habits. Turners subscribe to more newspapers than

[26] Civic affairs commemorating Germania's Old World heritage continued to be held at Turner Hall. (*New Ulm Review,* August 28, 1912, pp. 3–4). In 1912 a banquet held at Turner Hall marked the close of a week-long observance of the community's German heritage. Five thousand visitors from near and distant strongholds of German and Turner culture — Turner societies from St. Louis, representatives of every St. Paul German society — arrived on special trains in time to witness the main event, a parade consisting of four divisions, in the first of which marched "Hermann, the Cherusker, and six Teutonic warriors in the garb of the battle." Two representatives of foreign nations, accompanied by President Moersch of the German-American Alliance, were honored guests, the German consul, Hans von Grunow, representing Kaiser Wilhelm, and Edgar Proshnik, consul of Austria-Hungary. The German national anthem, "Lieb Vaterland," and the Austrian national anthem, "Gott erhalte den Franz den Kaiser," were played in honor of the distinguished guests. They were entertained during the week in the homes of two prominent citizens, a Turner and a non-Turner.

[27] Petry, *op. cit.,* pp. 17, 23.

[28] Gordon, *op. cit.,* p. 135. "The German-American community . . . was struck a sharp and powerful blow by the accumulated force of the passions generated by World War I — a blow from which it never fully recovered."

non-Turners, Members [T] taking more papers than anyone else and Non-Members [N-T] the least. The percentages of each group subscribing to one Sunday paper and to one or two daily papers are as follows: Founders [T] 76 and Members [T] 91; Settlers [N-T] 75 and Non-Members [N-T] 68. On the other hand, more Founders [T] (14 per cent) than anyone else (from 3 to 6 per cent) buy no newspapers at all.

Turners also subscribe to more non-German magazines and periodicals than non-Turners: 24 per cent of the first-generation Turners and 18 per cent of the second generation subscribe to seven or more magazines and periodicals, whereas fewer non-Turners — 11 per cent of each generation — take as many American magazines and periodicals. Turners average more subscriptions than non-Turners; the mean number of magazines and periodicals subscribed to by the households of each group are these: Founders [T] 4.6 and Members [T] 4.1, as compared with 3.4 for Settlers [N-T] and 3.3 for Non-Members [N-T]. Moreover, Turners and non-Turners do not read as frequently the same kinds of magazines. Though from four to six out of ten of the magazines taken by each group are of the kind that appeal to women — *Cosmopolitan, Better Homes and Gardens, Woman's Home Companion* — and though all groups subscribe heavily to four of the most popular national magazines (*Life, Look*, the *Saturday Evening Post*, and the *Reader's Digest*), Turners take these magazines more frequently than non-Turners (44 per cent of the Members [T], for instance, subscribe to these four national magazines, as compared with 14 per cent of the Non-Members [N-T]). In addition, Turners read more business and professional magazines (*Business Week, Changing Times: The Kiplinger Magazine, Successful Farming*, and the like) than non-Turners; and Founders [T] lead all others (by more than two to one — Founders [T] 28 per cent and Settlers [N-T] 13 per cent) in subscriptions to national news magazines such as *Time, Newsweek, U.S. News and World Report*, and the *Wall Street Journal*.

Similar results are obtained when comparing the average number of books owned by each group. The most striking differences fall at the extremes: 8 per cent of the Founders [T], no Members [T], and

24 and 22 per cent of the Settlers[N-T] and Non-Members[N-T], respectively, own fewer than ten books per family. At the opposite extreme (those who own more than seventy-five books) the proportions are Founders[T] 52 per cent and Settlers[N-T] 29 per cent; Members[T] 50 per cent and Non-Members[N-T] 19 per cent. No non-Turner estimates that he has more than three hundred and seventy-five books, while several Turner private libraries are considerably larger, some totaling as many as a thousand and three thousand volumes. The average Turner family has more than twice as many books as the average non-Turner family. Thus, in round numbers, the Founders[T] average three hundred books per family, Members[T] 115, Settlers[N-T] 75, and Non-Members[N-T] 45. Again, Turners do more serious reading than non-Turners (with the exception of religious books and magazines, which have less appeal for Turners). About twice as many Founders[T] as Settlers[N-T] (46 versus 22 per cent) own professional, educational, and technical books, or own and read the classics (42 versus 26 per cent). Member[T] versus Non-Member[N-T] differences are slightly less extreme. Turner versus non-Turner differences in the number and kind of books and magazines they read reflect different styles of life.

Style of Entertainment. Further evidence of Turners' status distinction emerges from an examination of their patterns of entertainment.

On the whole, Turners seek somewhat more highbrow forms of entertainment than do non-Turners. As evidence of their greater interest in classical music and jazz, more Turners than non-Turners own both FM radios and high-fidelity phonographs (12 per cent of each generation Turners, 6 per cent Settlers[N-T], and 3 per cent Non-Members[N-T]). This kind of music is almost unobtainable on local AM radio stations, and the more serious listener wants to hear it with high fidelity. Comparing the musical preferences of husbands and wives, Turner versus non-Turner, one finds direct confirmation of the foregoing generalization. The first generation prefers old-time music (the German polka and schottische) to any other, Settlers[N-T] more so than Founders[T], whereas the second generation much prefers popular or hit tunes. Non-Members[N-T], however, have more old-fashioned (Germanic) musical tastes than Members[T]—two to three times (up to 27 per cent) of the former as the latter prefer the old-time polka. Founders[T] alone show any sizable interest in classical music (30 per cent husbands and 22 per cent wives); the others show little interest (6 to 11 per cent) in good music. Turners' taste in music is more highbrow than the non-Turners'.[29]

This finding is not readily extended, however, to comparisons of Turner versus non-Turner television and motion picture viewing habits. Proportionately more Turners than non-Turners watch television less than three hours a week or not at all. (Almost everyone owns a set.) Comparing wives of respondents, one finds that though Members[T] and Non-Members[N-T] prefer the same kinds of television program, about half as many Founders[T] (22 per cent) as Settlers[N-T] (40 per cent) prefer quiz, comedy, and musical programs; and fewer Settlers[N-T] than Founders[T] (13 versus 20 per cent respectively) prefer some serious or dramatic television. No marked differences were discovered in program preferences of the husbands, however, western, mystery, detective, and sports programs hold more attraction for them than for their wives.

More Turners go to movies than non-Turners, the second generation attending with greatest frequency—22 to 27 per cent of Members[T] and Non-Members[N-T] are not patrons of movies, as compared with 48 and 66 per cent of Founders[T] and Settlers[N-T]. Comparing the motion picture preferences of the husbands, one finds little difference in the first generation: Founders[T] reveal slightly more interest in dramatic and musical movie themes than Settlers[N-T], but less than half of each group attends. Members[T], on the other hand, show a greater preference for comedy and drama (12 and 24 per cent) than Non-Members[N-T] (5 and 16 per cent). These differences do not appear among the wives, who here differ in only one respect: 3 per cent of the Member[T] wives, and 16 per cent of the Non-Member[N-T] wives, prefer musicals. In general, no

[29] Although a taste for classical music is "a German cultural trait differing significantly from the general American average," this alone does not explain the present Turner versus non-Turner differences. For, Turners are no more German culturally (and identify themselves even less with German culture) than non-Turners, who themselves do not represent the general American average.

clear motion picture preference is seen among the first generation, whereas for the second drama has most appeal.

Finally, Turners continue their traditionally active patronage of the arts — presently, concerts, symphonies, the opera, and ballet. The local community concert and high school play series offer Germania live entertainment, which Founders[T] attend most regularly. Over-all frequency of attendance at these events declines generationally from Founders[T] to Members[T], Settlers[N-T] to Non-Members[N-T]. For example, 32 per cent of the Founders[T] and 22 per cent of the Settlers[N-T] occasionally go to community concerts; 32 per cent of the Members[T] and 14 per cent of the Non-Members[N-T] occasionally attend local theatrical performances. Attendance at Twin Cities (Minneapolis–St. Paul, a hundred miles distant) opera, ballet, and symphony performances — more dependent on having time and money than is patronage of local concerts and theatrical performances — again shows this pattern. Though most (as above) do not attend, more Turners than non-Turners go occasionally or regularly: Founders[T] 24 per cent, Members[T] 15 per cent; Settlers[N-T] 9 per cent, Non-Members[N-T] 8 per cent. (The annual Twin Cities Beaux Arts Ball and the Governor's Ball are regularly attended by members of Germania society.)

Prestige. "Claims for prestige," observed C. Wright Mills, "are expressed in all those mannerisms, conventions, and ways of consumption that make up the styles of life characterizing people on various status levels."[30] The style of life of Germania's Turners evokes the bestowal of prestige upon them by those who do not or cannot make similar claims to honor. Such claims are based on birth and achievement. In Germania, where claims for prestige are not based on race and nationality, family assumes a basic importance. "Old families" receive noteworthy deference, and their occupational and educational achievements reinforce this deference.

Old-Family Associations. Almost one out of five Turners is related by birth or marriage to Germania's old families — 28 per

[30] "The Sociology of Stratification," in *Power, Politics, and People,* Irving Louis Horowitz, ed. (New York: Oxford University Press, 1963), pp. 310–311.

cent of the Founders [T] and 9 per cent of the Members [T], but only 9 per cent of the Settlers [N-T] and no Non-Members [N-T], while Turners generally are more closely associated with the old-family elite than non-Turners.[31] (It is worth noting in this regard that, with no exception, proportionately more Turners — in some cases twice as many — than non-Turners number among their personal acquaintances judges, physicians, lawyers, bankers, or manufacturers. Representative of this Turner versus non-Turner difference is the finding that though over four fifths of Founders [T] and Members [T] are personally acquainted with a judge, only about two fifths of Settlers [N-T] and Non-Members [N-T] claim to be.)

Turner versus Non-Turner familiarity and association with Germania's old families were compared. In every instance Turners know more old families and know them better than do non-Turners. Thus the percentages of each group which could name five old families are Founders [T] 70 and Members [T] 44; Settlers [N-T] 35 and Non-Members [N-T] 24. Conversely (and continuing the same order of comparison), the percentages which could not name at least one old family are 12, 21, 38, and 43. More Turners are better acquainted with more old families: over eight out of ten Founders [T] and approximately seven out of ten Members [T] know personally one or more old family members; about five out of ten Settlers [N-T], and four out of ten Non-Members [N-T] — many are newcomers in town — have formed such close association. Yet this is not the full story. When examining the nature of personal acquaintanceship that each group has with the old families, one finds that twice as many Turners as non-Turners are these families' good friends: 68 per cent of the Founders [T], but only 29 per cent of the Settlers [N-T]; and again, 35 per cent of the Members [T], yet scarcely 19 per cent of the Non-Members [N-T] are good friends of old families.

These observations are borne out by differences in the circumstances under which Turners and non-Turners associate with old

[31] The townspeople rated five families by prestige in response to the question: "Who are the five most widely known old families of New Ulm, in order of prominence?" First-generation respondents named three Turners in first, second, and fifth places; second-generation respondents named all Turners.

families and by the comparative frequency of their associations. Turners associate with old families on occasions more intimate and lasting than do non-Turners — such casual and nonbusiness affairs as drinking and dining together, either out on the town or in each other's homes. For instance, though non-Turners meet members of old families mainly in church or while transacting business, Turners (22 per cent Founders[T] and 41 per cent Members[T], but only 4 per cent Settlers[N-T] and 5 per cent Non-Members[N-T]) spend more of their leisure with old families. Furthermore, proportionately more Turners (from 6 to 18 per cent) than non-Turners (3 per cent) regularly dine with old families, and almost three times as many Turners (Founders[T] 24 per cent versus Settlers[N-T] 9 per cent) are in the habit of inviting members of old families, many of them relatives, to dinner.

Closeness to the Wealthy. It may be said that members of an enduring upper status group maintain their community standing partly by the judicious use of wealth. No status elite can hope to survive once its wealth is gone — some European once remarked that history is a graveyard of aristocracies. It is a commonplace that status elites have more money than ordinary people, spend much of their time with the rich, and know them well.

Founders[T] have more to do with the wealthy in Germania than has anyone else. The townspeople's knowledge of who are the wealthy and the frequency and closeness of their association were investigated. Turners and non-Turners were asked to name the five wealthiest families in town. Comparisons were made of the frequency with which names suggested by the respondents duplicated those on a prepared list of ten (which they were not shown). All groups, first and second generations, independently selected the same five names most frequently which corresponded closely to the first five on the ranked list prepared by the author. Furthermore, Turners and non-Turners arrived at almost identical rankings of the top five, all of whom are included in the aforementioned list of Germania's twenty-five wealthiest families.[32]

Comparatively fewer Founders[T] than anyone else (only 4 per

[32] See p. 86.

cent) admitted to not being personally acquainted with any of the wealthiest families of Germania; 15 per cent of the Members[T], and 13 to 32 per cent of the Settlers[N-T] and Non-Members[N-T] said they had no personal acquaintance with Germania's wealthy. Conversely, eight out of ten Founders[T] replied that they were personally acquainted with at least one of Germania's five wealthiest families, as compared with five or six out of ten Members[T], Settlers[N-T], and Non-Members[N-T] declaring personal acquaintance.[33] When one recalls that three of the five top families in Germania are Founders[T], these differences are understandable.

Club Membership. Prestige is gained by being seen at the right clubs, by taking part in worthy community causes, and most of all by assuming positions of leadership in civic and social affairs. Germania's high status groups move in a world of clubs. The social standing of each group with respect to the others may be partly determined by the number and nature of clubs and associations each frequents. For example, in Germania today the old elite are pulling out of the Lawn Club, which I was told is being overrun by the younger set, people with more pretensions than money or background.[34] (By 1965, eight or ten electric golf carts had made

[33] The complete tabulation of responses to the question "Do you know any of Germania's five most wealthy families personally?" is presented in Appendix Table 6.

[34] The Germania Lawn Club features dining, dancing, drinking, and golf. Wednesday night at the club is reserved for men. It begins jovially, after a leisurely afternoon's golfing, with cocktails before dinner, during which the day's game is reviewed, then a hearty meal of steak or lobster, eased with a final creme de menthe or martini, after which the men settle down to an evening of cards, dice, or conversation. Drinking continues until the late hours, animated by cards or dice for high stakes (seen less often these days) which only the wealthier members can afford. One seven-card gin rummy game held over two years before this study included bets of $50 a hand; some time before that dice games not uncommonly left a player as much as $2,000 ahead or out in a single night; a similar Wednesday "men's night," with dinner, heavy drinking, but no gambling, is an old Turner tradition. But much of this style of leisure is changing. New members of smaller means and modern habits are finding their way into the Lawn Club and the Turner Hall. Membership fees in both organizations, some believe, are too low, a mere $10 or $20 a year. And there are too few restrictions on membership, both clubs being open to the general public, although the Turnverein reviews and must unanimously approve each new member, who is sponsored by a Turner. However, unanimous approval is invariably approval by those few who attend a meeting for the introduction of new members.

their appearance at the Lawn Club. Costing $700 to $1,200 apiece, most of these have been purchased on time by young members whose annual incomes range from $8,000 to $10,000. An amusing example of the limits of local conspicuous consumption is the case of Clifford H. Nielson, a portly non-Turner in his late fifties whose legal practice allows little time for outdoor exercise. He recently bought an expensive golf cart. His exercise on the golf course drastically reduced, Nielson then had an electric exercise cycle installed in his office basement — and nearly lost a finger while trying to adjust the thing.) Those who make a point of joining clubs show their concern for their social standing.

Turners are socially outstanding in Germania. Their habit of devoting their leisure to clubs and associations is part and parcel of their prestigeful style of life. Turners exceed non-Turners in both out-of-town and local club memberships. (The Turnverein, far from being the Turners' own most esteemed organization, is but one of many — local, state, national — to which they are as strongly committed. The quickest guide to the active clubman in Germania, however, is Turnverein membership.) More Turners, both husbands and wives, have out-of-town memberships than non-Turners — the Founders [T] leading. (Turners, wealthier than non-Turners, have fewer working wives. Wives of the leisure class show their status by vigorous and well-publicized voluntary club work.) For example, comparing husbands: whereas 46 per cent of the Founders [T] and 41 per cent of the Members [T] hold memberships in one or more out-of-town clubs and associations, only 24 per cent of the Settlers [N-T], and 16 per cent of the Non-Members [N-T], do. (Although fewer of the wives hold out-of-town memberships, the Turner versus non-Turner difference is about the same: over twice as many of the former as the latter have such memberships.)

More Turner than non-Turner wives are members of three local (or locally represented) prestige associations: the Community Concert Society, the American Association of University Women, and the Great Books Club — named in the order of their increasing prestige. Though the differences are small, they are in the predictable direction; that is, the proportions of wives who are members of these three organizations are Founders[T] 32 per cent, Members[T] 24 per cent, Settlers[N-T] 22 per cent, and Non-Members[N-T] 13 per cent, a steady 10 per cent drop, from Turners to non-Turners, for each generational comparison.[35]

Even more striking differences are discernible when local club memberships are examined. Turners are by far the most active in Germania's club life: only 4 per cent of Founders'[T] wives belong to no club or association, fully 35 per cent of Settlers'[N-T] wives have no club affiliations. Less marked are the Member[T] versus Non-

Table 14. Husbands' Membership in Local Clubs and Associations

	Founder[T]	Member[T]	Settler[N-T]	Non-Member[N-T]
Member of at least 1 club	78%	82%	54%	51%
Member of no club	22*	18*	40	49
No answer	...	...	6	...
Total	100%	100%	100%	100%

*Other than the Turnverein.

Member[N-T] differences: a fifth of the wives of Members[T] and half of the wives of Non-Members[N-T] have joined no local club.

Turner versus non-Turner husbands' local club memberships are still more unequally distributed. More Turners are members of more clubs than non-Turners. One out of five Founders[T] (twelve in all, some with membership in more than nine clubs) claims membership in five or more local clubs and associations (including the Turnverein), whereas less than 4 per cent of the Settlers[N-T] (two exactly, each claiming six separate memberships) have joined as many clubs. Similarly, Members[T] are more active socially than Non-Members[N-T], for 35 per cent (twelve) of the Members[T] pay

[35] The top prestige society of Germania is the Junior Pioneers, which was until recently restricted to persons whose ancestors were original settlers of the community — Germania's answer to the D.A.R. Money is of no importance here — some members are all but impoverished. Turners and their friends are leading members of the society. But since 1965 the Junior Pioneers, last bastion of Germania's blooded aristocracy, has opened its doors to selected outsiders — much to the dismay of one first-generation descendant of the founders, an amateur historian now in his nineties, who resigned from the society in protest at the admission of the first such new member.

dues in more than five clubs, while only one (3 per cent) of the Non-Members [N-T] is a heavy joiner. When the groups are compared for membership in at least one local club (excluding Turnverein membership), the differences, shown in Table 14, are great.

In addition to holding more memberships than non-Turners, Turners occupy more leading positions in local clubs and associations. Both wives and husbands, first and second generations, hold directorships, presidencies, and other offices with about twice the frequency of non-Turners — husbands somewhat oftener than wives.

Table 15. Officeholding by Men in Local Clubs and Associations

	Founder[T]	Turner[T]	Settler[N-T]	Non-Member[N-T]
Officer in at least 1 club	30%	41%	11%	19%
Officer in no club	70	59	89	81
Total	100%	100%	100%	100%

The comparisons are shown in Table 15. Turners lead in civic and social affairs. Four of the five most active men in Germania's extrapolitical life — sponsors of a host of fund-raising drives, organizers of historic celebrations, chairmen of civic aid associations such as the Red Cross and the Blood Bank, and hometown boosters — are Turners. They have kept this leadership for two decades. Germania's most respected citizen (by virtually unanimous opinion) and former mayor, descendant of one of the town's oldest families, is a Turner. All of the five most active are self-employed, all earn well over $25,000 a year, two are prominent merchants, three are professional men.

Scale Analysis of Status

The status scale consists of items of behavior (e.g., association with old families, club membership), which provide a more direct and unambiguous basis for evaluating prestige than items of attitude or value.[36] Preserving the mode of scale analysis of the last chapter,

[36] No attempt has been made to assess the status aspirations of Turners and non-Turners of Germania. Since the concern here is to establish the degree of difference, if any, in class, status, etc., between Turners and non-Turners,

status scale scores have been divided into three frequency groups: high (scores from 49 to 65), medium (32 to 48), and low (scores ranging from 15 to 31).[37] When the frequency with which Turners and non-Turners achieved scores in these three groups is compared, the Turners show significantly higher status scores, as can be seen in Table 16.

Generational comparisons show that the wide status gap between the first generation has narrowed among the second. On the status scale, Founders[T] are unquestionably more prestigeful than Set-

Table 16. Turner versus Non-Turner Status Comparison *

Scale Category	Turner		Non-Turner	
	No.	%	No.	%
High (49–65)	14	18.7	3	4.2
Medium (32–48) ...	49	65.3	25	35.2
Low (15–31)	12	16.0	43	60.6
Total	75	100.0	71	100.0

*χ^2, Turner vs. non-Turner, $= 32.2$, 2 d.f., p$<$.001.

tlers [N-T], whereas Members'[T] prestige surpasses Non-Members'[N-T] by a somewhat narrower margin.[38] So high is the status score of Founders[T] that though they outrank Members[T] to a significant degree, Members[T] still exceed, in turn, the status score of Non-Members[N-T]. The status score of Settlers[N-T] is quite low, on the other hand, not significantly higher than that of Non-Members[N-T]. It is evident that relative to Germania's status hierarchy Members[T] are losing ground, Non-Members[N-T] gaining. Table 17 presents the essential comparisons.

Comparisons of scale scores between Members[T] and Non-Members[N-T] and between Settlers[N-T] and Non-Members[N-T] require that the measurement of their motives and mobility is of no direct relevance. These considerations have been taken up in the theory of the transformation of the ethnic community into status community form.

[37] The original scale was reduced from 16 to 15 items, the samples to Founders[T], 45, Members[T], 40, Settlers[N-T], 30, and Non-Members[N-T], 31. These adjustments were made to allow statistically significant comparisons of the groups. Rejected cases are analyzed on pp. 153–154; their exclusion does not appear to have appreciably altered the result.

[38] First and second generation units are compared. See pp. 19–20.

the scores be regrouped into two categories, high (41 to 65) and low (15 to 40), to produce sufficiently large cell frequencies for chi square analysis, as shown in Table 18. Scale results offer conclusive support of the hypothesis that Turners are the top status group of Germania. Statistical analysis based on fifteen status scale items yields significant differences between the prestige of Turners and non-Turners, but not between non-Turner generations (Settlers $^{N-T}$ and Non-Members $^{N-T}$). Less than once out of a thousand times would one expect to find Founders ^{T} outranking Settlers $^{N-T}$ (Table

Table 17. Generational Comparison of Status, Divided into 3 Groups *

Scale Category	Founder^T		Member^T		Settler^{N-T}		Non-Member^{N-T}	
	No.	%	No.	%	No.	%	No.	%
High (49–65)	10	22.2	4	13.3	2	5.0	1	3.2
Medium (32–48)	33	73.3	16	53.3	17	42.5	8	25.8
Low (15–31)	2	4.5	10	33.3	21	52.5	22	71.8
Total	45	100.0	30	100.0	40	100.0	31	100.0

*χ^2, Founder^T vs. Member^T, = 11.3, 2 d.f., p<.01. χ^2, Founder^T vs. Settler^{N-T}, = 25.9, 2 d.f., p<.001.

17) entirely by chance; less than twice out of a hundred times would chance account for the observed Member^T versus Non-Member^{N-T} status difference (Table 18). Today the Turners are ethnically indistinct from the non-Turners, but the Turners have retained their early status superiority.

Shifting Lines of Status

These findings have established on the one hand that though the style of life of the Turners reflects the perpetuation of "high culture" characteristics of an upper status group, *generational departures* from this style of life have taken place, and on the other hand that though Turners still claim and receive honor in Germania, the *terms of honor* are shifting: the elite are, as it were, under fire from upstart revolutionaires.

The findings show as well that there is status confusion in Germania, most diffuse among the younger generation. Not everyone knows his place or recognizes the local prestige groups. The prestige hierarchy is becoming a tissue of outmoded pretensions, conventions, or mannerisms; claims for prestige are not always acknowledged or understood; deference may be unexpectedly withheld, or given for the wrong reasons. Ambivalence and ambiguity are the best terms for the present situation.

Class in Germania has many faces, some new and hopeful, whose worth is plain even to the undiscerning, others older, more assured, who do not flaunt their riches. And so has status. Strolling about

Table 18. Generational Comparison of Status, Divided into 2 Groups*

Scale Category	Founder[T]		Member[T]		Settler[N-T]		Non-Member[N-T]	
	No.	%	No.	%	No.	%	No.	%
High (41–65)	28	62.2	15	50.0	9	22.5	5	16.1
Low (15–40)	17	37.8	15	50.0	31	77.5	26	83.9
Total	45	100.0	30	100.0	40	100.0	31	100.0

*χ^2, Member[T] vs. Non-Member[N-T] = 5.52, 1 d.f., p<.02. χ^2, Settlers[N-T] vs. Non-Members[N-T] = 0.14, 1 d.f., not significant.

town one meets both faces, though the encounter with each is more likely in some places than in others. In a residential section of Germania known locally as Mortgage Hill, the community's new hilltop suburb, houses are new, costly, and modern. The cheaper ones advertised for $15,000 are scattered apologetically amid the rest, which stand grandly for twice that, and more. Young faces, new in town, may be seen smiling around the backyard barbecues on a fair summer's day. Just out of hailing distance, southward along the bluff, stretched comfortably between the small Lutheran college that cuts off the suburb to the north and the Lawn Club at the cliff's edge to the south, is Summit Avenue. Old wealth is strung along Summit like a variegated strand of family jewels. It is spread along the casual drives that curve over spacious lawns, leading the eye to large old houses half hidden by weeping willows, rows of Russian olives, tall sentinel spruces. Their east windows, turned out toward the world, give one a view of Germania's wide, elm-lined streets,

119

ending abruptly at river's edge — in Goosetown — and of the bluffs beyond. Summit Avenue's wealth, proud and secure, is subdued; its glitter has faded, it lacks the dazzle and promise of Mortgage Hill. Inhabited by Settlers [N-T] and a few Founders [T], Summit's day is drawing to a close. Yet the day is long, the sun's course slow. So, too do the lengthening shadows of the Turners' day but creep across the land.

chapter 6

THE KALEIDOSCOPE OF POWER
IN GERMANIA

THE Turners, not surprisingly, exercise considerable influence in Germania. Power, wealth, prestige — these attributes commonly join to form a pace-setting combination of talents among an upper status group: "The power position of groups and of individuals typically depends upon factors of class, status, and occupation, often in intricate interrelations."[1] Turners are not alone, however, in the local arena of power and influence; other groups share in the maintenance of social order.[2]

Power: General Characteristics
Power, as here considered (and as it appears in Germania), is a multifaceted phenomenon, understood in terms of the varied means which different groups employ to exercise it and in terms

[1] Mills, "The Sociology of Stratification," in Horowitz, *op. cit.*, p. 315. See also Martindale, *American Social Structure*, p. 455. The relation of power to wealth and esteem is revealed in the clique and party structure of a status community. Parties are groups struggling for domination, as compared with classes, which seek goods and services. Status groups, on the other hand, monopolize prestige and jealously guard special styles of life. Thus the basic interests of these three types of social groups are different, though they may parallel one another in the same community. When they do, when there is a fusion of positions in the hierarchies of wealth, esteem, and power, there is a status community.

[2] Martindale, *American Society*, p. 364. "The terms we most frequently use for the bringing about of some kinds of actions and prevention of others (for the maintenance of social order) are *influence* and *power.*"

of their diverse ends. In the large sense, power, said Weber, is "the chance of a man or of a number of men to realize their own will in a communal action even against the resistance of others who are participating in the action."[3] Furthermore, Mills has suggested, "When we speak of the power of classes, occupations, and status groups . . . we usually refer more or less specifically to political power."[4]

Yet when we speak of the power structure of an existing community it is necessary that we extend the meaning of power to correspond with that reality: power has more than one form, and it may be exercised in extrapolitical ways by several competing groups.[5] Such competition is the situation in Germania today. Lasswell and Kaplan's ideal-typical construct of the forms and the base values of power is to the point; distinguishing eight forms of power arising out of eight corresponding values of two broad types, deference values and welfare values, they argue persuasively that power is always exercised in terms of one value or another.[6] A caution is added, however, by Martindale, who points out that in reality no single group completely monopolizes all or even any of the forms of power.[7] Since every group is itself a structure of power, affording its members access to certain scarce values, it is a mistake to assume that the problem is solved when, in a given community, a ruling elite alone wields decisive power. Community relations do not invariably crystallize into a single hierarchy of influence.[8]

Germania, composed of groups, presents overlapping structures

[3] Gerth and Mills, *Weber*, p. 180.

[4] "The Sociology of Stratification," in Horowitz, *op. cit.*, p. 316.

[5] This interpretation is basic to the pluralist view of community power, widely held by political scientists. Nelson W. Polsby, *Community Power and Political Theory* (New Haven: Yale University Press, 1963), pp. 112–121, summarizes the pluralist alternative to the power elite position.

[6] Harold D. Lasswell, and Abraham Kaplan, *Power and Society* (New Haven: Yale University Press, 1950), pp. 74–97.

[7] *American Society*, p. 366.

[8] Vidich and Bensman found, for example, that while in Springdale "a small number of individuals are engaged in a wide range of leadership positions," distinct spheres of influence and leadership – e.g., education and religion – prevail: "There are a great many leaders who are interested in and oriented to only one institutional sphere." See Vidich and Bensman, *op. cit.*, pp. 263, 271.

of power; each group, whether formed for primarily political, economic, religious, or social reasons, is itself such a structure. Moreover, no one of these groups has a single value base for the effective marshaling of its power. Certain religious groups exert political influence while socially prestigeful groups put economic pressures on other groups. The Turners, a complex political-social-economic group, have a variety of leaders who bring to bear different forms of power. Not all, by any means, are men of influence. From postal clerk and night watchman to manufacturer, lawyer, and surgeon, the Turners represent both extremes in the local array of occupational types. Some are wealthy but lack the prestige of others whose fortunes have dwindled or were never made. Some are politically hyperactive but have precious few old-family ties or no appreciable wealth. Others are virtually unknown outside their families and small circles of friends.

The assumption is here made that possessing wealth and property, holding professional and leadership positions in the occupational hierarchy, having a superior education, and associating with persons widely regarded as influential, constitute, in sum, the principal ingredients of power in Germania. Such an assumption does not require that one embrace "The theory . . . that affiliation with, or membership in, a social group engenders a certain homogeneity of belief and action which *may* lead to collective political action . . . the belief that the interests which unite the members of a social group and simultaneously divide them from other groups, are to the exercise of power what fuel is to fire" — a theory which Bendix himself, following Weber's analysis, does not agree with.[9]

No systematic attempt has been made in this book to find out what homogeneous beliefs, if any, characterize the Germania Turners. That they form an upper status group does not automatically imply any such homogeneity among them nor any concerted effort on their part to influence or dominate local politics. Fewer than two dozen Turners are men of community-wide influence. It is not at all clear, however, whether the small Turner leadership is itself in unanimous

[9] Reinhard Bendix, "Social Stratification and Political Power," in *Class, Status, and Power*, ed. by Bendix and Seymour Martin Lipset (Glencoe, Ill.: Free Press, 1953), p. 600.

accord on civic issues, joining forces to oppose any of the several non-Turner influence groups. Turnverein membership is much too heterogeneous — occupationally if in no other way — to allow a joining of forces on any but the most immediate concerns; for example, Turners agree practically to a man that their society must expand its membership and offer entertainment facilities to the general public in order to offset rising operating costs. They do not all agree, however, that Turnverein membership requirements have grown too lax, that their gymnastics program is badly in need of reviving, or that the Turnverein has "deteriorated" into a drinking club — complaints made from time to time by a discontented minority among the Founders [T]. Finally, it is doubtful — there are no instances known to me — whether the Turners would deliver a majority opinion on any major community issue: they were divided over the controversial school bond issue (see p. 134), though education has long been of prime concern to Germania's Turners.

What I am saying here is in effect that though the Turners as a group constitute an influential elite in Germania, there is no evidence that they therefore form a conspiracy of power.[10] Indeed, the idea would appear preposterous if not libelous to the Turners. If they are a true "power conspiracy," it is difficult to account for their failure to protect their own interests: for example, the town

[10] The conspiracy idea, a European import to American sociology, is seldom wholly applicable in North America. European observers of American politics who embrace some form of "power conspiracy" theory have on occasion made rather spectacular misstatements about American political events — for example, the rash of conspiracy interpretations of the assassination of President Kennedy. Among the more inane examples of this species of misapplied notions is Thomas G. Buchanan's *Who Killed Kennedy?* (London: Secker & Warburg, 1964), which first appeared in *L'Express* of Paris. Buchanan's analysis borders on the demonological. Even Bertrand Russell is not always immune to the temptation to see hobgoblins in high places. Appraising the Warren Commission Report, he said: "There has never been a more subversive, conspiratorial, unpatriotic or endangering course for the security of the United States and the world than the attempt by the U.S. Government to hide the murderers of its recent President." See *I. F. Stone's Weekly*, Vol. XII, No. 33 (October 5, 1964), p. 1. For discussions of the European origin and misapplications of the power elitism thesis, see Leon Bramson, *The Political Context of Sociology* (Princeton: Princeton University Press, 1961); Arendt, *Totalitarianism*, and Daniel Bell, *The End of Ideology* (Glencoe, Ill.: Free Press, 1960), pp. 43–67.

council voted in 1965 to withdraw the Turnverein's privilege, shared by a few other private clubs such as the American Legion Club, of keeping late closing hours. For years the Turnverein had kept its bar open seven nights a week as late as three o'clock in the morning or later, depending upon the occasion and the number of thirsty patrons (who let themselves in with keys). Germania's beer parlors and liquor bars (in all twenty), which by law must close at one in the morning, succeeded, despite Turner opposition, in obtaining a uniform closing time of 1 A.M., causing a drastic reduction in Turner Club liquor sales, traditionally heaviest after the downtown bars closed.

One could multiply examples of the limits on Turner power in Germania, which has dwindled steadily if gradually over the past fifty years. The point is perhaps obvious: the Turners are not *the* power elite of Germania. Other elites of influence in several institutional spheres exist. It is more reasonable to argue that some Turners have considerable influence (extending quite beyond the local scene), others very little; but on the whole their influence, due largely to the existence of a minority leadership within the Turnverein who are active in several capacities — educational, financial, religious, political, and social — is greater than that of the non-Turners.[11]

The following comparisons, which explore a variety of dimensions of power in Germania, support this view.

Local Political Activity

Turners lead a more vigorous political life than non-Turners. The former, both husbands and wives, show the greatest interest in local politics; about a fourth of the wives of Founders[T] (12) say they take an active part in Germania's political affairs; the wives of Settlers[N-T] and Members[T], however, are completely inactive politically, and only two (5.4 per cent) wives of Non-Members[N-T] stir themselves to political action. Turner husbands as well are most active politically: 32 per cent of the Founders[T] as com-

[11] Hence power in Germania does not conform to Mills's vision of interlocking institutional command posts; *Power*, pp. 5–6.

pared with 7 per cent of the Settlers [N-T], 6 per cent of the Members [T] but only 3 per cent of the Non-Members [N-T], are so involved.[12]

Turners are more conscientious about their political responsibilities than non-Turners: 10 to 20 per cent more of the Turners, husbands and wives in both generations, than of the non-Turners vote regularly in local elections (for the town's mayor, six members of the school board, and five city council members). For example, 94 and 91 per cent of male Founders [T] and Members [T] claim they always vote in these elections; 76 and 78 per cent of male Settlers [N-T] and Non-Members [N-T] make this claim.[13] As might be expected, Turners are the leading holders of public office in Germania: about a fourth of the Founders [T] are or have been officeholders, as compared with 9 per cent of Members [T], 7 per cent of Settlers [N-T], and 8 per cent of Non-Members [N-T]. Proportionately almost four times as many Founders [T] as Settlers [N-T] hold political office in Germania. The political involvement of the second generation is statistically identical, and low.

In many towns and cities of North America labor union membership is for workers a means of exercising political power. In Germania it is not. Close to 90 per cent of the male working population of Germania does not belong to a labor union — 84 per cent of the Settlers [N-T], 89 per cent of the Non-Members [N-T]. Nine out of ten Turners are not union members. (Half of the Founders [T], slightly over a third of the Members [T], we recall, are proprietors or professionals; very few are skilled or unskilled workers.) Germania is not a union stronghold.

Though union membership does not identify those with influence in Germania, association with local political officials does. Turners still have more friends and relatives in public office than non-Turners; 58 per cent of the Founders [T] and 44 per cent of the Members [T] acknowledge that they have close friends and relatives

[12] See pp. 19–20 for a description of the samples compared in this study.

[13] Seymour Martin Lipset, *Political Man* (New York: Doubleday, 1960), pp. 179–186. In his discussion of who votes and why, Lipset argues that mere conscientiousness in community politics — regular attendance at meetings and so forth — does not demonstrate that a group has political power. On the contrary, it may mean that highly developed political responsibility is a sign that a group is well educated.

who are (or recently have been) elected or appointed officials in Germania — members of the city council, incumbents of the offices of mayor, sheriff, and city manager, and the chief of police. Considerably fewer non-Turners — about 3 out of 10 Settlers [N-T], 2 out of 10 Non-Members [N-T] — have friends and relatives in public office.[14]

The Turners' greater involvement in local politics and closer association with politicians and public officeholders are extended also to state and national spheres: half of the Founders [T] but only a fifth of the Settlers [N-T] have two or more friends and relatives active in either the DFL or the Republican Party. (Fewer Members [T], but still more than Non-Members [N-T] — 29 versus 11 per cent respectively — have such associations.)

Political Confidence

Familiarity breeds confidence as well as contempt. Fuller, more familiar participation in local politics appears to have made the Turners, especially the second generation, confident of their political influence and ability. Non-Turners are less confident. Dahl contends that persons sure of their ability to understand and informally influence local politics have political influence; this argument underlies the following analysis.[15]

First, Turners are more inclined than non-Turners to feel that they have an effective informal voice in local government. The proportions of those who are so persuaded are Founders [T] 80 per cent, Settlers [N-T] 75 per cent — apparently the majority do not admit to having only formal political influence — Members [T] 91 per cent, and Non-Members [N-T] 68 per cent. Members [T] are most confident that their voice counts.

Second, about half the Founders [T] and a third of the Settlers [N-T] believe that their influence on local government is not restricted to the vote. More of the second generation — Members [T] 56 per cent

---

[14] In Germania today the office of mayor carries no decisive political power and little prestige. The mayor does not lead; in reality he is only a figurehead; compare, for example, Vidich and Bensman, *op. cit.*, pp. 270–271.

[15] Robert A. Dahl, *Who Governs?* (New Haven: Yale University Press, 1961), pp. 282–301.

and Non-Members [N-T] 49 per cent — suspect that their political influence extends beyond the formal exercise of voting.

Third, and showing the same trend, though 68 per cent of the Founders [T] and 62 per cent of the Settlers [N-T] feel that local political officials are responsive to their opinions or serve their interests, fully 88 per cent of the Members [T] but only 60 per cent of the Non-Members [N-T] agree that what they think carries weight with Germania's politicians.

Finally, Turners are most confident of their ability to fathom local political issues: over eight out of ten Founders [T] and all but one Member [T] rejected the suggestion that local politics is a mystery to them, whereas about seven out of ten Settlers [N-T] and close to eight out of ten Non-Members [N-T] (again the second generation shows greater political confidence than the first) feel that town politics is within their grasp.[16]

These findings, however, are by no means conclusive. It may be that the first generation, especially the Founders [T], have retired from active politics because for them the rewards of officeholding have become inconsequential. They may exercise what power they possess elsewhere or behind the scenes. One thing is certain: they are not so publicly prominent in Germania politics today (few Turners hold public offices in town) as they once were. There are no Turners on the city council, and only six Turners are city officials. There are eighty-five positions in all, and only one Turner occupies a prominent office, as municipal judge.

Influential Associations, Local and Extra-Local

Those who do not hold official jobs with influence may exercise power indirectly, provided their friends are in strategic positions. The respondents were asked to name the three most influential citizens of Germania,[17] and all names submitted were tallied and ranked according to frequency. Of the five families mentioned most often, four are Founders [T] and one is a Settler [N-T]. Turners themselves are most familiar with Germania's influential families, for

[16] See questions 86–89, Appendix 3.
[17] Respondents were instructed to regard "influential" in terms of ability to force decisions on significant public issues.

more Founders[T] (78 per cent) than Settlers[N-T] (58 per cent) — but about the same number of Members[T] (71 per cent) and Non-Members[N-T] (68 per cent) — were able to name at least two of the three most influential families of Germania.[18] Conversely, about a fifth of the Founders[T] but close to two fifths of the Settlers[N-T] were not able to name correctly a single family of outstanding influence in Germania.

In addition, more often than they named others, the Turners named themselves as having much influence: 54 per cent of the Founders[T] said that of the three most influential families in Germania two were Turners, whereas only 29 per cent of the Settlers[N-T] agreed with them (35 per cent each of Members[T] and Non-Members[N-T] made this claim).

Most respondents revealed by their answers that power is, or is believed to be, contingent upon wealth in Germania. The first generation feel most strongly that this is so. The respondents included three of Germania's wealthiest families among the five they considered most influential. Even those two less wealthy families among the five, ranked first and third in terms of influence, are each worth between $100,000 and $200,000 in total capital investments.[19]

[18] A prepared list of the ten most influential families of Germania, based on my intimate knowledge of the community, was used as the basis for evaluating the accuracy of each respondent's selection. Over all, the community evaluation closely parallels mine, though the second generation, more than the first, tended to confuse political position with political influence.

[19] Turner Heinrich Ottenstroer, rated most influential by the community, is widely admired for his civic zeal. He is Germania's number one booster, occupies leading positions on all major committees, holds memberships in virtually all non–Roman Catholic clubs and organizations. The townspeople say that he has done more for Germania than any other person of his generation; he is in his fifties. In 1964, he was selected as one of one hundred outstanding Minnesotans by the "Minnesota U-S-A Rally," and honored at a "Republicans Care" awards luncheon at the Sheraton-Ritz Hotel in Minneapolis. Those who receive this award "are people who, because they firmly believe in accomplishing good and progress at the local level, best epitomize the four 'I's' of the 'I Care' awards program — Integrity, Idealism, Initiative, and Individualism," said Raymond Plank, chairman of the Minnesota U-S-A Rally. (See New Ulm *Journal Review*, February 14, 1964, Section 1, p. 4.)

Public spirited, a regular churchgoer, he adheres to conservative political views. He is a member of the Junior Pioneers, the Brown County Historical Society, the Minnesota Good Roads Association, the New Ulm Development Association, past member of the city council, charter member of the Boy Scouts of America, life member of the Minnesota State Historical Society, past

The other three are worth from $500,000 to $6,000,000 in gross investments. No member of these five outstanding families holds a political or public office in Germania.[20]

Table 19. Personal Acquaintance with 3 Most Influential Families

	Founder[T]	Member[T]	Settler[N-T]	Non-Member[N-T]
Know personally all 3 families	72%	50%	27%	13%
Know fewer than 3 of the families ..	12	21	26	30
Do not know any ..	16	29	47	57
Total	100%	100%	100%	100%

Personal acquaintance with Germania's influential families is itself a mark of power. The percentages of those who know personally three of the ten most influential families of Germania are shown in Table 19.

The attorney in American society has unusual influence. His legal skill and political connections are most commonly exercised

president of the New Ulm Chamber of Commerce, for many years director of the Minnesota Employers and Minnesota Taxpayers associations, former president of the city charter commission and of the Germania Turnverein, and chairman or member of several other civic and business associations; he serves on the Governor's Committee of 100 for promotion of new industry in Minnesota and is a Mason and a Shriner. He votes Republican and detests socialism; has no intellectual interests, and though a staunch officer of the Turnverein he does not share its utopian traditions. (But then, neither does anyone else.) In short, Ottenstroer epitomizes the small businessman in North America who, true child of free enterprise, lives out his life in the shadow of the great corporation.

The political conservatism of Germania's leadership, incidentally, is well known to the townsmen — and a source of dismay to the liberal minority. In 1958, for example, three prominent citizens, members and advisers of the Centennial Committee, and leaders of the local press and radio and television stations, insisted that the community invite Senator Joseph McCarthy as the principal guest speaker for the celebration. Sober voices succeeded in defeating the idea, arguing that the invitation would stand as a disgrace to Germania's reputation.

[20] This is hardly surprising; officeholding in Germania today, as in small towns across the nation, is a tiresome business. Indeed, that finding has become a sociological commonplace. For example, Vidich and Bensman (*op. cit.*, p. 278) state: "A number of small businessmen occupy formal leadership positions, but it is precisely they who are not the real leaders." Dahl (*op. cit.*, pp. 282–301) found that in New Haven high-status people had all but abandoned party politics.

in the interests of the powerful. In Germania the Turners make fullest use of the power of the attorney. Over five to almost seven out of ten respondents believed that if one were involved in some kind of serious trouble in Germania the best person to know would be an attorney. (Only about 3 per cent thought a priest, business-man, physician, banker, or the mayor or district judge would be of any real assistance in time of trouble.) Turners, who felt most strongly about this, are most likely to retain their own lawyer, as Table 20 suggests.

Table 20. Percentage Retaining a Family Lawyer

Response	Founder[T]	Member[T]	Settler[N-T]	Non-Member[N-T]
Have own lawyer ..	72%	62%	49%	40%
Do not have own lawyer	24	38	46	57
No response	4	...	5	3
Total	100%	100%	100%	100%

Table 21. Percentage Who Named a Turner as the Best Person to Know in Case of Trouble

Respondent	Founder[T]	Member[T]	Settler[N-T]	Non-Member[N-T]
Turner	66%	35.3%	21.8%	29.7%
Non-Turner ..	14	23.5	40.0	45.9
Other*	4	14.7	12.7	8.1
No response or don't know ...	16	26.5	25.5	16.3
Total	100%	100.0%	100.0%	100.0%

*Lawyer or clergyman.

Many respondents — at least one out of five — named a Turner as the best person to know in time of trouble. The percentages who selected a Turner are shown in Table 21.

The high rate of selection of Turners — there are only a hundred and twenty-two in a population of twelve thousand — leaves little doubt that some members of the Turnverein are inordinately influ-ential. In fact, of those Turners regarded as most important to know — and there are only six in all — three are lawyers. With the exception of the Founders[T], all those who named a Turner named a lawyer, and 62 per cent of the Founders[T] concurred.

Scale of Analysis of Power

It was predicted that the outstanding class and status characteristics of the Turners lead to and support greater opportunities for exercising local influence. Scale analysis again affirms the descriptive findings.[21] Tables 22–24 summarize the situation in 1962. Generational comparisons of power scores show that Founders[T] outrank Settlers[N-T], but Members[T] are scarcely more influential than Non-Members[N-T]. Regrouping power scale scores into two frequency categories, high (40 to 66) and low (13 to 39), one arrives at Table 24's generational comparisons.

Hence, on the basis of scale results, Turners remain more influential than non-Turners. Statistically, the probability is less than once in a thousand that Turners exercise greater persuasive power than non-Turners purely by chance. Though Founders[T] are preeminently influential, Turners' dominance is waning: the power score of Members[T] is not significantly greater than the power score of Non-Members[N-T].

The Interplay of Power

Power is changing hands in Germania. New and wider arenas of influence now accommodate more numerous and diverse interests — newly arrived manufacturing interests, for example, are bringing new power into the arenas. Increasingly the Turners have felt the persistent nudge of non-Turner interests and the insistent claims of competing voices bidding for a larger share of local political capital. Since 1900 it has been plain to the astute observer that two contesting hierarchies of civic, political, and religious influence were coalescing, one Roman Catholic and the other Protestant.

Some of the Turners have moved into the upper ranks of the

[21] See Appendix 2, p. 165, for power scale items. Power is phrased in the scale in terms of the nature and frequency of interaction with persons considered influential by the respondents and by me. Power is also identified with membership in influential organizations — including national organizations with local chapters — with the holding of public office, and with the subject's own estimate of his political effectiveness.

Table 22. Turner versus Non-Turner Power Comparison *

Scale Category	Turners No.	%	Non-Turners No.	%
High (49–65)	24	30.8	7	9.0
Medium (31–48) ...	45	57.7	38	49.4
Low (13–30)	9	11.5	32	41.6
Total	78	100.0	77	100.0

*χ^2, Turner vs. non-Turner, $= 22.7$, 2 d.f., $p<.001$. The power scale was reduced from the original 14 to 13 items. For purposes of statistical analysis the samples were shortened to Founders[T] 46, Members[T] 32, Settlers[N-T] 41, and Non-Members[N-T] 36. See pp. 154, 158 of the Appendixes for an analysis of the rejected cases.

Table 23. Generational Comparison of Power, Divided into 3 Groups*

Scale Category	Founder[T] No.	%	Member[T] No.	%	Settler[N-T] No.	%	Non-Member[N-T] No.	%
High (49–65)	18	39.1	6	18.8	6	14.6	1	2.8
Medium (31–48)	21	45.7	24	75.0	22	53.7	16	44.4
Low (13–30)	7	15.2	2	6.2	13	31.7	19	52.8
Total	46	100.0	32	100.0	41	100.0	36	100.0

*χ^2, Founder[T] vs. Settler[N-T], $=7.6$, 2 d.f., $p<.05$.

Table 24. Generational Comparison of Power, Divided into 2 Groups *

Scale Category	Founder[T] No.	%	Member[T] No.	%	Settler[N-T] No.	%	Non-Member[N-T] No.	%
High (40–66)	34	73.9	14	43.7	14	34.1	7	19.5
Low (13–39)	12	26.1	18	56.3	27	65.9	29	80.5
Total	46	100.0	32	100.0	41	100.0	36	100.0

*χ^2, Founder[T] vs. Member[T], $= 6.03$, 1 d.f., $p <.02$. χ^2, Settler[N-T] vs. Non-Member[N-T], $= 1.41$, 1 d.f., not significant. χ^2, Member[T] vs. Non-Member[N-T], $= 3.62$, 1 d.f., not significant.

latter hierarchy; none has a key position in the former. Other Turners have influence outside Germania — in state and federal government and in far-flung professional associations.[22] As the local struggle for domination in town and school politics continues, the older Turners withdraw and concentrate their energies on extra-local spheres.

Meanwhile, one hears dark predictions of a Roman Catholic usurpation of power in Germania, sparked perhaps by the creation in 1957 of the Diocese of Germania and the subsequent construction in 1960 of a $750,000 chancery, home of the bishop and of the central governing body of seventeen counties.[23] There is evidence to suggest that the reins of power in Germania are being taken up by Roman Catholics. For instance, the ill-fated public school bond issue, calling for the construction of a $2,500,000 high school, was defeated twice in 1962 for two reasons: townspeople objected to an increase in taxes, and the Roman Catholic element feared that their influence in local education would be weakened.[24]

[22] For example, a few Turners are, or have been, on visiting terms with state senators and representatives; several are members of the American Bar Association (one is a business partner of a past president of the Association who is also a member of the International Academy of Trial Attorneys); Turners hold offices in the American Medical Association, and membership in the Medical College of Surgeons; some are members of the Minnesota Club in St. Paul, others of the Minneapolis Athletic Club. Prominent Turner physicians associate with the internationally renowned Mayos of Rochester. One or two Turner attorneys move with ease in the upper rank of state politics, or have a friend (one living in Germania is listed in *Who's Who*) with a line to the capitol.

[23] *New Ulm Pioneer*, 1858, No. 1 (trans. by Mrs. William Durbahn). Roman Catholic stock has risen sharply since the year 1858, when the town's first newspaper, Turner inspired, railed against the clergy: "Cannot every idle simpleton, every spiritual rascal, become a priest if he is lazy and brash enough to make a business of the falsehoods and such immorality . . . to stand before the spiritually minded people to quack ecclesiastically?" Then in language heavy with sarcasm, the *Pioneer* commented on the recent flurry of religious enterprise in Germania, concluding: "The church enterprise grew like mushrooms in the idle excitement, and fanatical stupidity took courage. Priests ran to and fro. . . . We will keep an eye on the originators and scrutinize their future aims and behavior."

[24] The Roman Catholic hierarchy, informants say, believes that the Germania school board (to which their incumbent, a Catholic, was not re-elected) is opposed to them, and that they had to show their strength by blocking the school bond issue, though eventually they will cooperate. (A new high school is badly needed.) It is rumored that the bishop exhorted his

Mills's formulation accurately catches the mood of the ascendant Catholic stratum: "The accumulation of political power by any stratum is generally dependent upon a triangle of factors: willful mentality, objective opportunity, and the state of organization."[25]

Power in Germania is not stratified in a single overarching hierarchy. Rather, multiple interpenetrating hierarchies of influence prevail. For example, the religious hierarchy, dominated by Roman Catholic and Lutheran contingents; the long-established merchant-banking-manufacturing hierarchy, its leadership currently being challenged by the new professionals — production and sales managers, engineers, cost accountants, and the like — of post–World War II arrivals such as International Milling & Supersweet Feeds, Kraft Foods, B. F. Goodrich, Minnesota Mining and Manufacturing, and Tachtronic instruments (manufacturing Servo Motors and Moto Tachometers for government military contracts); and the professional hierarchy, comprising lawyers, doctors, dentists, accountants, ministers, and teachers, many long outstanding in the community.

All exert influence in various directions: the religious leadership, for instance, wields political as well as religious influence sometimes greater than that of the business establishment. A dramatic confrontation between the two occurred a few years ago when the religious leaders succeeded in discontinuing, for the time being, the annual July Polka Day, a festive and profitable occasion initiated by the main street merchants and heralded as the revival of an old German tradition. Visited by ten thousand to thirty thousand merry-

parishioners on the eve of the first school bond election to vote against it, asking if they personally were content to eat hamburger while, at their expense, the rest of the community dines on steak. As of July, 1962, the Catholic element had succeeded in delaying the expansion of the public school system. But not for long: on January 8, 1964, Germania sold $1,950,000 in bonds for the new senior high school, let contracts July 9, 1964, to three local firms for almost $1.7 million, and broke ground July 21, 1964. Completed in 1966, the new building will help to accommodate the rapidly rising school population; up 6.6 per cent in 1963–1964, and 78 per cent over the 1951 population by 1964, public school enrollment was almost 2,000 in 1964, total school enrollment near 5,000 by the 1964–1965 school year. The total cost of school construction during 1964 was $2.7 million, a record year. New Ulm *Journal Review*, February 14, 1964, Section 1, p. 2.

[25] Mills, *Power*, p. 316.

makers (customers to Germania's merchants), who drank enormous quantities of beer and danced past midnight in the streets to the thumping music of over a dozen old-time bands situated on every downtown street corner, Germania on Polka Day began, after a few years, to look like the scene of a latter-day bacchanalia — until the outraged religious leadership stepped in. Despite strong arguments by local merchants that profits during Polka Day generously compensated them for damage and inconvenience, the religious leaders persuaded the city council to cancel the next Polka Day.

It is by now apparent that this book presents no incontrovertible evidence in support either of the view that power is completely pluralist or that it is monolithically hierarchical. The study of power in contemporary American sociology has coalesced into two essentially polar positions, sometimes referred to as the pluralist and the hierarchical views.[26] The Turners of Germania have long since ceased to occupy the apex of a local pyramid of power,[27] though historical evidence suggests that they once did — but not in this century (see Chapter 4). The power situation in Germania today inclines rather more toward the pluralist model than the hierarchical, but does not exemplify either in pure form.[28]

The main purpose of this chapter, however, has not been to reveal the nature of power as such (or its quality in Germania), but rather to show how it joins with wealth and prestige in the hands of an upper status group. Though political leadership in Germania is slipping out of the Turners' hands, this trend does not invalidate the hypothesis, confirmed by descriptive and statistical evidence,

[26] See Thomas F. Anton, "Power, Pluralism, and Local Politics," *Administrative Science Quarterly*, Vol. VII, No. 4 (March, 1963), pp. 425–457; Nelson W. Polsby, "Three Problems in the Analysis of Community Power," *American Sociological Review*, Vol. XXIV, No. 6 (December, 1959), pp. 796–803; and Raymond E. Wolfinger, "Reputation and Reality in the Study of 'Community Power,'" *American Sociological Review*, Vol. XXV, No. 5 (October, 1960), pp. 636–644.

[27] Floyd Hunter's conception of power in Regional City allows for "gaps in the power arc," that is, for "*pyramids* of power." Cf. *Community Power Structure: A Study of Decision Makers* (Chapel Hill: University of North Carolina Press, 1953), pp. 61–62.

[28] A great many studies of community power have been launched from pluralist and elitist perspectives. Two notable studies may be taken as illustrative of each respective point of view: Dahl, *op. cit.*, and Hunter, *op. cit.*

that by re-forming into a strategically placed status group the Turners of Germania have easily stepped into positions of influence, supplying for several decades the active leadership of the community. Only with the second native-born generation, those who have reached maturity since the Second World War, is it clear that Turner leadership has passed its peak.

IV

Summary and Conclusion

¶ *chapter* 7

THE TURNERS' RETREAT FROM
MONOPOLY

GERMANIA, U.S.A., is no longer its own town, if ever it was, and
it has ceased to be a "Turner town." The pace of the change that
has swept the world since Germania was founded — just two years
before the publication of Darwin's *Origin of Species* and Marx's
Critique of Political Economy, and from today's perspective the
world of 1857 was another, more constant world — has spared few
communities, however small or remote. Only a careful cataloguing
and skillful ordering of the regional, national, and international
events of the past century could recreate the story of Germania's
transformation from a frontier outpost into a vigorous trading and
manufacturing center. In some measure, however, this story is available to special internal analysis as well as selective historical reconstruction of Germania's past and present. It is not necessary to
know everything in order to know something is the rationale of
this, and every, piece of scientific investigation.

The Turners have had a great deal to do with Germania's history,
even if it cannot be said that they have ever had command of it.
Having rescued the rude original settlement from oblivion, they
guided its first steps toward economic and political solvency, where-
upon they built their hall — long the focus of town gatherings —
and busied themselves with consolidating their initial advantage.

They drafted a city charter, organized a school system, commanded the defense of the town during the Sioux uprising, and installed their members as president, justice of the peace, mayor, city clerk, treasurer, city attorney, city engineer, city councilman, and in numerous other offices. Turners became prominent in the medical and legal professions. They saw several of their friends and members elected to state office: secretary of state, treasurer, senator, and representative. The founder of Germania, William Pfaender, was one of the first presidential electors from the state of Minnesota. Horace Austin,[1] active in the defense of Germania in 1862, became a governor of Minnesota, serving from 1870 to 1874. Thus for several decades Germania could be called a Turner town. After the 1860's, the arrival of non-Turner settlers — who soon outnumbered the Turner founders ten to one — changed all that. The effect on the Turners was two-fold: their cultural heritage, German and Turner, fell into neglect, and they became a leading status group.

Events like these have been theoretically understood as general processes of community formation and change by Weber, MacIver, Martindale,[2] and others, and given more precise expression by Don Martindale, whose secondary principles of ethnic and status community formation supply the basic explanation of this book. These principles, which summarize the features of ethnic and status minority relations with the majority community, generated the two main working hypotheses of this book: 1. The historical and cultural experience of the Turners who founded Germania accounts for their initial formation as an ethnic community. 2. The superior social, political, and economic situation of the Turners accounts for their subsequent re-formation as an upper status community.

Scale Findings

The two general and the four specific working hypotheses of the book are confirmed by historical, contemporary descriptive, and statistical findings. Statistical verification of the four specific hypotheses has rested on the scale analysis; the scale findings, summarized in Table 25, confirm all predictions.

[1] Not a pseudonym.

[2] Cf. Gerth and Mills, *Weber*; MacIver, *Community, op. cit.*; and Martindale, *American Social Structure*.

The Turners' Status Consolidation

It is evident that the dimension of power, ignored by Warner and his associates, and the distinction between class and status group, buried in the concept of social class, are of primary importance in the foregoing analysis of the Turners as a status community. All three dimensions — class, status, and power — combined and monopolized in the status community, have been indispensable to under-

Table 25. Summary of the Scale Findings

Scale	Prediction	Actual Result
Class	Turner > non-Turner	$\chi^2 = 16.3$, p<.001, confirmed
Status	Turner > non-Turner	$\chi^2 = 32.2$, p<.001, confirmed
Assimila- tion	No difference	$\chi^2 = 1.2$, not sig., confirmed
Power	Turner > non-Turner	$\chi^2 = 22.7$, p<.001, confirmed

standing the position and experience of the Turners in Germania — to their forming a status community in the first place. The consolidation of power, wealth, and esteem in the status community is deftly explained in the following quotation:

The community-forming principles of completeness and closure operating with respect to access to esteem, wealth, and power tend to consolidate the three types of values in the same hands and freeze access to them to the in-group. No matter where one starts, with high esteem, great wealth, or superior power, the other dimensions tend to be added. . . . High rank in one respect tends always to consolidate its position by achieving complementary rank in others. Moreover, once high rank is consolidated in all three dimensions it leads on toward closure. The positions in the highest of the social hierarchies tend to be monopolized first.[3]

The Turners are a case in point of the kind of consolidation of access to power, wealth, and prestige seen in an upper status community. Their transformation from an ethnic to a status community has meant the extension of these spheres of value for them. Thus by becoming a status subcommunity in Germania the Turners have broadened and heightened their prestige from the limited stage of the ethnic community to the wider arena of the local, and to some

[3] Martindale, *American Social Structure*, p. 455.

extent, the national community.[4] In the same way they have enhanced their positions in the hierarchies of wealth and power. Changes in the Turners' life chances have been traced on the basis of their access to these values.[5]

As Germania lost its small-town insularity, however, the Turners were displaced somewhat, and found it necessary to share influence with contesting groups. Whether the broad movement from elitism to pluralism in Germania since the turn of the century represents the typical "power drift" in American small towns is a question requiring further study.[6]

Germania Faces the Future

Turners' prominence in Germania, still evident to old residents, has, chameleon-like, taken on new coloration to overcome the risks of change. They are not nearly so outspoken, for example, about religion — few are avowed freethinkers, none are publicly atheists, as once they were.[7] More Turners are Roman Catholics than ever before. Many years ago an unspoken arrangement was

[4] Gerth and Mills, *Weber*, p. 188. Weber discusses the manner in which the status community may eventually achieve a legal codification or support of its newly won honor: "The development of status is essentially a question of stratification resting upon usurpation. Such usurpation is the normal origin of almost all status honor. But the road from this purely conventional situation to legal privilege, positive or negative, is easily traveled as soon as a certain stratification of the social order has in fact been 'lived in' and has achieved stability by virtue of a stable distribution of economic power."

[5] *Ibid.*, p. 194. For example, economic changes of national as well as local or regional origin may in time alter the fortune of the Turner status community — if they have not already. "Every technological repercussion and economic transformation threatens stratification by status and pushes the class situation into the foreground," observes Weber.

[6] See Mills, "The Structure of Power in American Society," in Horowitz, *op. cit.*, p. 25. If, as Mills has argued, "the history of modern society may readily be understood as the story of the enlargement and the centralization of the means of power," this process begins in large national organizations. Its effect on the power structure of small towns is likely to be upsetting, to say the least; as, for example, when a large national firm builds a plant in a small town, hiring local workers but importing managerial and professional persons, who by their occupational identification with the wider society and their expertise present a competitive image which may well disrupt whatever local monopoly of influence has prevailed. See also Vidich and Bensman, *op. cit.*, pp. 91–102.

[7] See Appendix Table 15 for the religious composition of Germania.

worked out between the lay and religious leadership of Germania; it has rarely been disturbed.[8]

Though the Turnverein is Germania's most active displaced institution — as the townspeople say, there is always something going on at Turner Hall — Turners themselves, as individuals, do not go unnoticed. A tabulation of the number of Germania Turners mentioned in the 1941 and 1958 editions of *Who's Who in Minnesota*,[9] as compared with the numbers of non-Turners so mentioned from the county (Germania is the county seat) and from Germania reveals a striking fact: the percentage of non-Turners is decreasing, while the percentage of Turners is increasing.[10] Turners' prestige is not inconsequential: in 1958, two out of five citizens of Germania listed in *Who's Who in Minnesota* (and 73 per cent of all those in the county so listed were residents of Germania) were Turners, an increase of 15 per cent over 1941. Turners continue to receive unusual public recognition.

Though these findings appear to contradict the main thesis of the study, they actually lend additional support to it. The increase in Turner prominence is, significantly, extra-local. Precisely those Germania Turners mentioned in *Who's Who in Minnesota* are not actively engaged in local politics, do not depend upon local patronage and good will for their success in business and the professions, and hold memberships in more state and national associations than the ordinary townsman. Moreover, they are a small minority of the existing body of Turners. That Turners continue to be outstanding locally and that they have won increased recognition outside Ger-

---

[8] Indications are, however, that the traditional Turner insistence on the separation of public and parochial education has weakened. In August, 1965, for example, the New Ulm Board of Education reversed its former stand on the issue of "shared time," voting 5 to 1 in favor of educating ninth grade parochial school students in agriculture. The single dissenting vote was that of a Turner member of long standing, who expressed his concern over what he called the shaky legality of his own position!

[9] Esther Stutheit, ed. (Minneapolis: Minnesota Editorial Ass'n, 1942; Bernice White, ed. (Waseca, Minn.: Brown Printing Company, 1958). The foreword to the 1958 edition states: *"Who's Who in Minnesota* is a recognition of service to mankind, and not of financial prominence, unless accompanied by consideration of an obligation to humanity."

[10] See Appendix Table 16 and p. 154 for a discussion of these findings.

mania does not necessarily mean they constitute a dominant leadership in the community.

The Implications of Growth

Meanwhile, Germania's future seems unusually bright. Currently riding the crest of national prosperity, the community has seen a spate of building projects, the establishment of new industries and the construction of new houses, as well as the improvement and enlargement of existing facilities, educational, religious, business, civic, and social. A three-million-dollar addition to Germania's municipal power plant, doubling its size, was completed in 1964–1965. By October, 1964, permits had been taken for eighty-one houses valued at $1,105,500 (above the sixty-nine permits of 1963, valued at $906,000, though less than the record one hundred and thirteen houses built in 1959 at a total cost of $1,224,800); for thirty-eight industrial and commercial buildings, totaling $3,333,938; and for various civic and educational construction, one hundred and ninety-five permits at a combined value of $1,230,495. In all, $5,669,933 was spent on building construction alone in Germania during the first ten months of 1964, which exceeded the largest previous expenditure of the past decade by about $2 million.[11]

An impressive part of this record volume of construction has been supplied by national firms, which present a challenge to Turner elitism. Today Germania's industrial colony, numbering thirty-two manufacturing and processing firms ranging from cabinet-making and brewing to the manufacture of burial vaults, duplicating machinery, and road building equipment, includes five representatives from the five hundred largest corporations in the United States: National Dairy Products (parent company of Kraft), Borden's, B. F. Goodrich, Minnesota Mining and Manufacturing, and International Milling. National Dairy ranked in 1964 twenty-second in national sales. With the exception of Borden's, all have entered Germania since 1950, two as recently as 1959 and 1962. Minnesota Mining and Manufacturing spent $1 million on a new plant in 1964

[11] Figures supplied by the New Ulm Chamber of Commerce (October, 1964) and by the New Ulm *Journal Review*'s "Progress Edition" (February 14, 1964), Section 1.

— the largest single industrial construction that year — and in 1963, 3M equipment expenditures were about $56 million and its research and product development expenditures more than $30 million in the company's two plants on Germania's north side.

Not one Turner has investments or holds a supervisory position in any of these five local plants. (Three, one a new member of the Turnverein, hold skilled and semiprofessional jobs in two firms: a laboratory technician at 3M, a printer and a chemist at International Milling. Three others, the remainder, hold unskilled and semi-skilled jobs: a plating operator at 3M, a production worker and a guard at Kraft.) Typically, the managerial, supervisory, and technical staff of these postwar plants consists of outsiders brought in by the parent companies. All six of the local plant managers have been transferred to Germania from larger urban centers, four within the past five years. Most Turner proprietors and managers, by contrast, are shopkeepers and small manufacturers, many running businesses established by their fathers and grandfathers.

Three of the thirty-two firms in Germania in 1964 were owned and operated by Turners, employing one hundred and three of the fourteen hundred and eighty workers in all firms. Six firms, representing by far the greatest combined investment in Germania and employing eight hundred workers living within a radius of thirty miles, are branch plants of national corporations. The remaining twenty-three locally owned non-Turner firms employ five hundred and seventy-seven workers.

In little more than a decade, and with mounting effect in the past few years,[12] the percentage of employees in Germania's six national manufacturing and processing firms had grown in 1964 to just over half (fifty-four per cent) of the total. By comparison, in the same year, the locally owned non-Turner firms employed thirty-nine per cent, whereas the Turner-owned firms employed seven per cent of the fourteen hundred and eighty workers.[13] The inundation of national non-Turner business investment shows no sign of reversal.

[12] For example, B. F. Goodrich more than doubled its volume of sales from its first year in Germania, 1960, to 1964; 3M anticipated an increase of from 160 employees in 1965 to 250 by the spring of 1966.

[13] It is noteworthy, however, that in 1964 the 121 Turners, representing

The Persistence of Turner Influence

For the time being, however, several of Germania's richest Turners, in business and the professions, remain in a position to take considerable advantage of the community's current prosperity: of the seven general contractors in town, the largest and oldest, owned and managed by a Turner, won bids for over $1,261,000 of all construction during 1964; two of the five plumbing companies, including the largest, are owned by Turners; similarly, two of the three local lumber companies are under Turner control; of the two breweries, which have both been in continuous operation for over a century, the larger is owned by a Turner and Turners are vice president and secretary of the smaller (both sell to a five-state area); Germania's only bus company is owned and operated by Turners, as is the only laundry and drycleaning plant in town (which draws 63 per cent of its business from out of town and has been run by the same family for fifty years); two other Turners enjoy local business monopolies, one owns a music store and the second a salvage company; Turners own one each of the two monument companies, two paper companies, and two nurseries in Germania. Finally, Turners own and operate two each of the three photography studios and three undertaking establishments in the community.

Turner professional men continue to be numerous. For example, two of the three medical clinics are owned by four Turners (there are twelve doctors in Germania). The Turner physicians have three associates altogether, which makes Turners and their associates numerically dominant in local medical circles. Moreover, the chairman of the mental health board of the proposed three-county mental health center, under construction in Germania in 1966, is both a Turner and the town's wealthiest individual doctor. The local animal hospital is owned by the wealthier of two veterinarians, a Turner. The richest lawyer is a Turner (three of the fifteen lawyers in town are Turners); a Turner dentist lives in one of Germania's finest and oldest houses.

about 3.3 per cent of Germania's population (at an average of 3.5 residents per household), employed 7 per cent of these 1,480 workers, whereas the 12,306 non-Turner majority (96.7 per cent of the population) employed the remaining 93 per cent.

There can be little doubt, therefore, that as a group the Turners of Germania are still outstanding in business and in the professions. And they remain fairly cohesive; in view of the finding that the Turners are a status elite, it is no surprise to learn that Turners employ Turners: fourteen in business establishments and five at the Turner Club. The predominance of Turner firms with up to four members of the family holding jobs in them partly accounts for their economic cohesiveness.

Nevertheless, Germania's growing dependence on outside industry, its partial loss of autonomy to powerful national political institutions, and its expansion of non-Turner interests all point to the eventual decline of the local Turner elite. They have lost much of their old monopoly and are more and more feeling the competition of prestigeful agents of the wider society.[14]

The advantages of life in a status community give a peculiar tenacity to its existence. Nothing like it is seen in the ordinary ethnic community where, in the United States at least, powerful forces of assimilation exert a steamroller effect on its unique formation. The Turners of Germania neatly escaped this fate by very early grasping the lesson of life in a complexly structured society: there is safety in monopoly.

Others, too, appreciate this tactic, forming, often unwittingly, monopolies of their own. Germania's future hinges partly on the outcome of the various bids for power, wealth, and prestige which Turners and non-Turners are now making. But this is not all, or even, perhaps, at all important: in reality, Germania's fate — political, economic, and even, it seems, physical — is balanced on the same scale that weighs nations and gives an accounting of governments, the scale of power and humanity, between which hang the life and death of civilization.

[14] See Don Martindale, *Institutions, Organizations, and Mass Society* (Boston: Houghton Mifflin, 1966), pp. 524, 535. Martindale suggests that "The world of the large-scale organization shatters the circles of primary groups and the small community." The formation of the American national community has led to a new national stratification system. Consequently the "old types of strata," which include the workers in local family firms, the entrepreneurs, and "the descendants of the families founded by the entrepreneurs," are broken up and forced aside by the corporate men of large-scale organizations.

Appendixes

¶ appendix 1

TABLES AND ANALYSES OF
REJECTED CASES

T H E mean capital worth of each group was calculated by taking the mid-value of each category (i.e., for the capital worth category $30,000–$50,000, the estimated value is $40,000), adding all amounts of more than $1,000, and dividing by the total number of respondents who claim any capital investment, whether more or less than $1,000. This procedure was adopted to produce a fair estimate of the mean capital worth of the majority of each group. The results are summarized in Appendix Table 5.

Class Scale. The rejected cases of each sample were inspected to determine whether their retention would have altered the results. Appendix Table 7 compares (1) the mean number of scale items each group did not answer, (2) the mean scale score of rejected cases for each group, and (3) the mean scale score of included cases for each group. Large differences in a direction opposite to the findings would suggest that by rejecting several cases in each group the results may have been reversed. This does not appear to have happened in the analysis of class: both the rejected and the included Turner cases are higher than the non-Turner cases.

Assimilation Scale. Comparing rejected and included cases in the same way as was done for the class scale, we find that the inclusion of the former would not appreciably alter the results. If anything, non-Turners' assimilation scores would be somewhat higher than Turners' if all cases were included in the scale analysis. Appendix Table 10 presents the relevant comparisons.

Status Scale. Although over a fourth of the Settlers [N-T] were excluded from the final scale analysis, a comparison of rejected and included cases shows that reducing the sample sizes has not biased the results. Those Settlers [N-T] and Non-Members [N-T] not included in the scale analysis received mean scale scores five and six points lower than the excluded Turner samples. Appendix Table 13 presents a comparison of rejected and included cases.

Power Scale. The power scale findings would not be reversed were the fourteen rejected cases from the subsample of Settlers $^{N-T}$ included in the final analysis. On the contrary, as Appendix Table 14 shows, the lowest-scoring part of the Settlers $^{N-T}$ have been omitted; their inclusion would have produced even greater differences between Turners and non-Turners.

In 1941 one out of four men from Germania (25.6 per cent) who were included in *Who's Who in Minnesota* was a Turner (they make up 13.4 per cent of all those in *Who's Who* from the county). In 1958, exactly two out of five – an increase of about 15 per cent – of those listed from Germania were Turners (they were 21 per cent of the county population included in *Who's Who*). Since 1941 the majority of the residents of the county listed in *Who's Who in Minnesota* have been Germanians: 52 per cent in 1941 and 73 per cent in 1958. Yet the proportion of the county's population living in Germania was in each case less than the percentage from Germania listed in *Who's Who*: in 1940, there were 8,743 Germanians in the county population of 25,532; in 1960 the figures were 11,114 and 27,676. One can only conclude that on the whole the population of Germania is unusually prestigeful and that a few of the Turners among them enjoy a high and mounting public acclaim. Appendix Table 16 summarizes these findings.

Appendix Table 1. Comparsion of Mean Ages of Husbands and Wives

	Founder ^{T}	Member ^{T}	Settler $^{N-T}$	Non-Member $^{N-T}$
Husband	57.7	36.5	57.2	32.3
Wife	56.3	34.7	54.1	25.6

Appendix Table 2. Two-Generation Comparison of Wife's Occupation

Occupational Category	Founder ^{T}	Member ^{T}	Settler $^{N-T}$	Non-Member $^{N-T}$
Proprietor and professional	18%	5.9%	7.3% *	16.2%
Managerial and semiprofessional	. . .	2.9	. . .	8.1
Clerical and sales	10	26.5	14.5	13.5
Skilled	2	. . .	3.6	8.1
Unskilled	68	61.8	72.7	54.1
No information	2	2.9	. . .	. . .
Total	100%	100.0%		100.0%

*Total not equal to 100 because of rounding.

Appendix Table 3. Comparison of Occupations of the Fathers
of Founders[T] and Settlers[N-T]

Occupational Category	Founders' Fathers (N = 50)	Settlers' Fathers (N = 55)
Proprietor and professional	36.0%	7.3%
Managerial and semiprofessional	8.0	10.9
Clerical and sales	8.0	5.5
Skilled	14.0	10.9
Unskilled	32.0	60.0
No information	2.0	5.5
Total	100.0%	100.0%

Appendix Table 4. Numbers and Percentages of Turners and
Non-Turners Who Claim Capital Investments

Response	Founder[T]		Member[T]		Settler[N-T]		Non-Member[N-T]	
	No.	%	No.	%	No.	%*	No.	%
Capital worth >$1,000	35	67.3	21	61.8	19	34.5	9	24.3
Capital worth <$1,000	16	30.8	10	29.4	29	52.7	23	62.2
No response	1	1.9	3	8.8	7	12.7	5	13.5
Total	52	100	34	100	55		37	100

*Total not equal to 100 because of rounding.

Appendix Table 5. Total and Mean Capital Investments of
Turners and Non-Turners

Value	Founder[T] (N = 51)	Member[T] (N = 31)	Settler[N-T] (N = 48)	Non-Member[N-T] (N = 32)
Range*	$5–$250	$5–$89	$3–$400	$7.5–$68
Total capital investment	$2,967,000	$682,000	$1,031,000	$188,000
Arithmetic mean	$58,178†	$22,000	$21,480	$5,875

*Rounded to the nearest $1,000; amounts are in thousands of dollars.
†If the entire $7,000,000 inheritance of the potentially wealthiest Founder[T] were included in the calculation, the mean would be $180,725.

Appendix Table 6. Personal Acquaintance with 5 Wealthiest Families

Response	Founder[T]		Member[T]		Settler[N-T]		Non-Member[N-T]	
	No.	%	No.	%	No.	%	No.	%
Acquainted	40	80.0	20	58.8	33	60.0	20	54.1
Not acquainted ...	2	4.0	5	14.7	7	12.7	12	32.4
No response	8	16.0	9	26.5	15	27.3	5	13.5
Total	50	100.0	34	100.0	55	100.0	37	100.0

Appendix Table 7. Comparison of Rejected and Included Cases of
the Class Scale

Finding	Founder[T]	Member[T]	Settler[N-T]	Non-Member[N-T]
Rejected	21.2%	23.5%	23.6%	15.6%
Mean no. of items	(N = 11)	(N = 8)	(N = 13)	(N = 5)
unanswered	2.0	1.8	1.5	2.4
Mean scale score of				
rejected cases	28.0	30.3	26.5	24.0
Mean scale score of				
included cases	36.6	35.7	29.6	30.3
	(N = 41)	(N = 26)	(N = 42)	(N = 32)

Appendix Table 8. German and Non-German Ethnic Origin
of Husbands and Wives

	Founder[T]		Member[T]		Settler[N-T]		Non-Member[N-T]	
Ethnic Origin	Husband	Wife	Husband	Wife	Husband	Wife	Husband	Wife
Not German ..	8%	20%	6%	24%	14%	9%	16%	16%
Part German .	6	10	21	24	13	18	30	35
All German ..	86	66	71	50	71	71	54	49
No infor-								
mation		4	2	2	2	2	...	...

Appendix Table 9. Percentages with Personal Acquaintances in Germany

No. of Germans Known	Founders[T]	Members[T]	Settlers[N-T]	Non-Members[N-T]
One	8%	6%	71%	70%
Two or more*	40	35	27	30
None	44	59	2	...
No information	8	...	...	...
Total	100%	100%	100%	100%

*The ranges in numbers of Germans known are as follows: Founders[T],
2–500; Members[T], 2–7; Settlers[N-T], 2–25; and Non-Members[N-T], 2–5.

Appendix Table 10. Comparison of Rejected and Included Cases of the
Assimilation Scale

Finding	Founder[T]	Member[T]	Settler[N-T]	Non-Member[N-T]
Rejected	26.9%	8.8%	16.4%	2.7%
Mean no. of items	(N = 14)	(N = 3)	(N = 9)	(N = 1)
not answered	1.4	1.7	1.1	1.0
Mean scale score of rejected cases	19.1	13.3	19.4	20.0
Mean scale score of included cases	22.1	19.0	22.3	17.6
	(N = 38)	(N = 31)	(N = 46)	(N = 36)

Appendix Table 11. Generational Comparison of Assimilation, in 3 Groups

Scale Category	Founder[T] No.	%	Member[T] No.	%	Settler[N-T] No.	%	Non-Member[N-T] No.	%
High (31–41)	3	7.9	..	...	7	15.2	..	...
Medium (20–30)	21	55.3	10	32.3	21	45.7	12	33.3
Low (9–19)	14	36.8	21	67.7	18	39.1	24	66.6
Total	38	100.0	31	100.0	46	100.0	36	99.9

Appendix Table 12. Generational Comparison of Assimilation, in 2 Groups

Scale Category	Founder[T] No.	%	Member[T] No.	%	Settler[N-T] No.	%	Non-Member[N-T] No.	%
High (26–41)	8	21.1	2	6.5	15	32.6	2	5.6
Low (9–25)	30	78.9	29	93.5	31	67.4	34	94.4
Total	38	100.0	31	100.0	46	100.0	36	100.0

Appendix Table 13. Comparison of Rejected and Included Cases of
the Status Scale

Finding	Founder[T]	Member[T]	Settler[N-T]	Non-Member[N-T]
Rejected	13.5%	11.8%	27.3%	16.2%
Mean no. of items	(N = 7)	(N = 2)	(N = 15)	(N = 6)
not answered	5.6	2.5	5.0	3.5
Mean scale score of rejected cases	24.3	20.0	19.3	14.0
Mean scale score of included cases	43.1	37.2	32.1	26.1
	(N = 45)	(N = 32)	(N = 40)	(N = 31)

Appendix Table 14. Comparison of Rejected and Included Cases of
the Power Scale

Finding	Founder[T]	Member[T]	Settler[N-T]	Non-Member[N-T]
Rejected	11.5%	5.9%	25.5%	2.7%
	(N = 6)	(N = 2)	(N = 14)	(N = 1)
Mean no. of items not answered	2.5	1.0	2.4	5.0
Mean scale score of rejected cases	26.0	38.5	18.5	8.0
Mean scale score of included cases	45.0	40.2	35.0	31.5
	(N = 46)	(N = 32)	(N = 41)	(N = 36)

Appendix Table 15. Religious Composition of Germania's Men*

Religion	Founder[T]		Member[T]		Settler[N-T]		Non-Member[N-T]	
	No.	%	No.	%	No.	%	No.	%
Protestant	31	62	24	71	33	60	20	54
Roman Catholic	10	20	9	27	20	37	16	43
Other†	9	18	1	2	2	3	1	3
Total	50	100	34	100	55	100	37	100

*The religious affiliations of wives and husbands are almost identical.
†Includes atheist, agnostic, freethinker, Jewish, and "None."

Appendix Table 16. Turners and Non-Turners in *Who's Who in Minnesota*,
1941 and 1958

	1941				1958			
	County		Germania		County		Germania	
	No.	%	No.	%	No.	%	No.	%
Turners	20	13.4	20	25.6	10	21.0	10	40.0
Non-Turners	129	86.6	58	74.4	38	79.0	25	60.0
Total	149	100.0	78	100.0	48	100.0	35	100.0

Sources: *Who's Who in Minnesota*, Esther Stutheit, ed. (Minneapolis:
Minnesota Editorial Association, 1942); Bernice White, ed. (Waseca, Minnesota: Brown Printing Company, 1958).

STRUCTURAL AND GENERATIONAL
PROBLEMS OF GERMANIA: Method of Study

THE two broad hypotheses which guided the study of social change in Germania required somewhat different methods of study. Since the Turners who founded Germania came from strata not naturally inclined to withdraw into segregated ghettos, it was hypothesized that special forces must have been at work if such segregation took place. The existence of such forces can only be established by historical investigation of the background of the Turners.

The Historical Investigation of Germania. The historical reconstruction of the key features of their background has three sources: general histories of the Turners in Germany and in North America; particular histories of their community by the Turners in Germania; and a variety of source materials (journals, newspapers, diaries, letters, census and other statistical reports, and the recollections of older Turners now living in Germania). The records and publications of the social and cultural organization of the Turners, the Turnverein, provide an added source of information.

Experimental Design for Study under Field Conditions. The second general hypothesis maintained that though Germania started out as an ethnic community, it turned into a status community after all. This hypothesis concerns forces that are still very much a part of the living reality of Germania. A somewhat different mode of approach is required. For this purpose an ex post facto design for study under field conditions was deemed most effective.[1]

[1] An experimental design of this type has been analyzed by Ernest Greenwood (*Experimental Sociology: A Study in Method*, London: King's Crown Press, 1945) and extensively developed for sociological research by F. Stuart

Two samples were chosen, an experimental group of Turners and a control group of non-Turners. The selection of these two sample groups presented no unusual problems. All available male members of the Germania Turnverein — that is, all Turners living in Germania who could be reached during the course of the interviewing — were included in the sample. The Turnverein consists of both Club members and regular Turnverein members — the former, in contrast to the latter, being for the most part non-Turners, who have neither voting privileges nor formal rights in the organization. Club members who enter the Turner Hall primarily for recreational reasons — they numbered about 450 in 1965 — do not have the Turner tradition, and have therefore been excluded from the Turner sample.

The total membership at the beginning of the summer of 1962 was 121 (exactly the 1965 membership). Though then classified as "active" (dues-paying) members, 2 of the 121 were seriously ill (and are now deceased), and three others were not interviewed for personal reasons, though they gave valuable aid in getting information and answering questions pertaining to the study. These deletions brought the total active membership to 116. For one reason or another, 30 could not be interviewed, reducing the experimental sample to 86.

A sample of the non-Turner population of Germania was needed to compare the distinctness of the Turners (primarily in class, status, and power) and in order to help follow the changes that have occurred in their lives. The control sample was gathered from the total non-Turner population of Germania, both German and non-German. Several steps were taken to ensure a wide selection, resulting in an initial list of 140 Germanians, of whom 92 were interviewed.

The control sample was selected from the 1961 edition of *Polk's City Directory*, 201 pages long, listing Germania's 12,000 population. Of the 201 pages, 140 were chosen at random, providing a basis for then selecting, by a table of random numbers, 1 name from each page (of from about 20 to 35 separate entries), making in all a total sample of 140. All members of the Turnverein were excluded from the directory beforehand, as were all names that did not apply

Chapin (*Experimental Designs in Sociological Research*, New York: Harper, 1947, pp. 95–139). Chapin declares (p. 95) that the basic approach of the ex post facto design is "a description of the *present situation as an effect* of some previously acting causal factors and attempt to trace back over an interval of time to some assumed causal complex of factors which began operating at an earlier date."

to the study (rural residents, children, and unmarried residents except widows). When an inapplicable name was randomly selected, the standard procedure was either to take the name of the father, when the name of a child had been drawn, or to take the next relevant name on the list for each page sampled.

In addition to a Turner versus non-Turner comparison to determine the relevant differences between them, first and second generations of each sample were compared to discover the changes that had occurred during the past few decades within the Turner status community. By contrasting two generations of Turners with two generations of non-Turners, it was possible to identify further the direction in which the Turners, as a status community, were moving. A question that will be answered by a generational comparison is Do the sons of Turners have more or less influence in Germania than do the sons of non-Turners? It is expected, for example, that in the process of becoming a status community the Turners extended their influence to the entire community, while at the same time they began to lose much of their ethnic and ideological distinctiveness, as Germans and as Turners, identifying themselves with the wider society as Americans. Generational comparisons are needed to disclose the precise nature of these changes. The two generations compared in the present study consist of Turners and non-Turners, those 45 and above, and those below age 45.

Technical Problems. In addition to the procedural problems of the study, the second hypothesis presents a number of technical problems. Basically, they involve the development and validation of an instrument to isolate and quantify the aspects of change in the Turner status community, from the first to the second generation, as well as the differences between Turners and non-Turners. The instrument, a pre-coded questionnaire,[2] was constructed in two parts, one part consisting of semistructured items for making general comparisons between the groups, the other comprised of scaled items selected to make the four aspects of the study operationally identifiable: *class, status, power,* and *assimilation.*

The Research Instrument. The precise determination of differences between Turners and non-Turners and changes from generation to generation in the four main variables — class, status, power, and assimilation — can be facilitated by the development of valid scales. The core of the research instrument designed for the present study consists of four scales, each constructed to represent operationally a variable for predicting and testing differences between

[2] The questionnaire is reproduced in Appendix 3.

the experimental groups. Two major problems arise in building the instrument: scale formation and scale validation.

The Formation of the Scales. The development of scales of class, status, power, and assimilation was pioneered by several students of social stratification in American sociology and anthropology (see Part III). My analysis is an extension of their enterprise.

The Class Scale. It was proposed that class can be determined by a scale of objective items designed to assess four general characteristics: occupation (the source of income), amount of income, education, and possessions or property. No attempt has been made to rate class subjectively or psychologically, as has been done by many researchers (Gallup, Cantril, and Centers, for example).[3] Too often this approach yields imprecise results — the great majority of those interviewed assigned themselves to the middle classes, or class and status were confused.[4]

The inclusion of education in a scale of class finds support in the high positive relation between income, occupation, and education.[5] Possessions or property form a basic index of class; it takes money to acquire material goods.[6] Gerth and Mills point out that

[3] See G. Gallup and S. Rae, "The Pulse of Democracy: The People of the United States — A Self-Portrait," *Fortune*, February, 1940; H. Cantril, "Identification with Social and Economic Class," *Journal of Abnormal and Social Psychology*, Vol. XLVIII (January, 1943) pp. 74–80; and R. Centers, "Social Class, Occupation, and Imputed Belief," *American Journal of Sociology*, Vol. LVIII (May, 1953) pp. 543–555.

[4] Both Hollingshead and Warner have conducted subjective ratings of class. Hollingshead's procedure, a refinement of Warner's Rating by Matched Agreements plus Rating by Comparison, is ostensibly geared to rating status, but it includes criteria of class (income) as well. (Hollingshead, *op. cit.*, p. 29.) In Warner, Meeker, and Eels, *op. cit.*, p. 35, Warner's Evaluated Participation procedure is highly subjective; its success rests on the assumption that the members of a community are well aware of the rank of those around them. However, only in a small stable community does it seem possible to apply the method of EP with any degree of precision.

[5] Joseph A. Kahl, *The American Class Structure* (New York: Holt, Rinehart, and Winston, 1957), p. 97. Kahl observes, for example, that "men who finished college earn 150 per cent more than the grammar school group", and "even within any given occupation, the men with more education make a little more money." See also Egon Ernest Bergel, *Social Stratification* (New York: McGraw-Hill, 1962), pp. 272–276, who suggests that contrary to the generally held argument that education is dependent on class, a good case can be made to prove the opposite.

[6] Max Weber, "Social Stratification and Class Structure," Talcott Parsons *et al.*, eds., *Theories of Society* (Glencoe, Ill.: Free Press, 1961), Vol. I, pp. 573–576. This forms the basis for Weber's first type of class (p. 573), a "property class" — "primarily determined by the differentiation of property holdings" — as compared with an "acquisition class" and the more general concept of "social class."

in the United States today "occupation rather than property is the source of income for most of those who receive any direct income."[7] Since Germania's Turners, bearers of a strong entrepreneurial tradition, have been particularly inclined to improve their class position by acquiring property, this index is deemed an indispensable part of the class scale.

The scale designed to assess class situation is composed of the following items: 1. Occupation (past or present) of wife; 2. Present occupation of husband; 3. Formal education of wife; 4. Formal education of husband; 5. Rent or own a house; 6. If house owned, approximate value; 7. Amount of property owned; 8. Number of cars owned; 9. Year of newest (or only) car; 10. Joint yearly income; 11. Capital worth; 12. Acquaintance with wealthy families; 13. Number of "top ten" wealthy families named.

Items 1 through 6 on this scale of class compare favorably with eight of the nineteen indices compiled by Kahl and Davis[8] in their study of the intercorrelations between social class stratification indices taken mainly from the Warner and North-Hatt scales and census categories. The remaining seven are additional measures of class, covering the amount of income and possessions or property as well as association with the rich.[9]

Responses to all scale items were distributed on a five-point continuum, representing a rank order of positions.[10] All items, of whatever range of responses, have been coded by scores 1 to 5; in some cases this has necessitated grouping the responses into five categories, forming ordinal scales. In addition to ordinal scales, however, the instrument contains some quasinominal (or partially

[7] Gerth and Mills, *op. cit.*, p. 312.

[8] Joseph A. Kahl and James A. Davis, "A Comparison of Indexes of Socio-Economic Status," *American Sociological Review*, Vol. XX (June, 1955), pp. 317–325. Kahl and Davis, who found "relatively high positive correlations" between the nineteen different items of social stratification, suggested that two variables underlie most of the items: (1) occupational position and (2) quality of the house and residential area. Their factor analysis indicated, as Hatt had shown, that the best single index of social class is occupational position. (Paul K. Hatt, "Occupation and Social Stratification," *American Journal of Sociology*, Vol. LV (May 1950), pp. 533–543.)

[9] Membership in an upper status group would naturally mean frequent associations with the wealthy. Acquaintance with upper-class individuals is therefore deemed an index of a man's own class position.

[10] The present development of scales follows the usage of Alex Simirenko (*op. cit.*) in a study of a Russian ethnic community. His scales are patterned after the "Mandel Social Adjustment Scale" (Nathan G. Mandel, "Social Adjustment Scale Manual," unpublished; Minneapolis: Department of Psychiatry Research, University of Minnesota, 1959).

ordered) scales.[11] For example, item 2 on the class scale is partially of the nominal type: [12]

> Occupation of husband
> Proprietor/professional
> Managerial/semi-professional
> Clerical/sales
> Skilled
> Unskilled

In scales of this nature there is no implication that the responses indicate more or less of the characteristic being measured,[13] though the example given exhibits features of the ordinal scale as well, showing the positive relation between occupational level and class position.

Item 10, on the other hand, is of the ordinal type: [14]

> Joint income
> $12,000 and over
> $10,000–$12,000
> $8,000–$10,000
> $5,000–$8,000

On this scale the responses are arranged in order of more or less of the characteristic (income) being measured, with no specification of the distance between positions: "An ordinal scale defines the relative position of objects or individuals with respect to a characteristic, with no implication as to the distance between positions."[15] Since responses to all scale items represent the relative possession of class, status, power, or assimilation traits, the scales are basically of the ordinal type. Scale scores have been assigned to the responses for each item, forming the basis for computing (by χ^2) differences between the samples.

The Status Scale. Status was determined on the basis of scores received on scale items: 1. Attendance at community concerts; 2. Attendance at theater plays; 3. Germania prestige club membership; 4. Out-of-town club membership, wife; 5. Out-of-town club membership, husband; 6. Local club membership, wife; 7. Local

---

[11] Claire Selltiz et al., *Research Methods in Social Relations* (New York: Holt, Rinehart, and Winston, rev. ed., 1961), pp. 189–193.

[12] See pp. 168–174.

[13] Selltiz, *op. cit.*, p. 189. "A nominal scale is one that consists of two or more named categories, into which objects or individuals or responses are classified."

[14] See p. 169.

[15] Selltiz, *op. cit.*, p. 191.

club membership, husband; 8. Position held in local clubs, wife; 9. Position held in local clubs, husband; 10. Personal acquaintances of prestigeful occupation; 11. Number of old families named; 12. Acquaintance with old families; 13. Acquaintance with top five of old families; 14. Extent of acquaintance with old families; 15. Nature of association with old families; 16. Frequency of association with old families.

The primary basis for selecting items that reveal prestige by Germania's standards is the author's knowledge of the community as a former resident (1939–1953) and the insights of other long-time residents of Germania, especially those of high status, who served as informants. The experience of other students of status phenomena has also guided the present formation of a status scale adapted to the peculiarities of Germania, U.S.A.[16]

The Power Scale. Power in Germania was operationally specified and explored by a scale of fourteen items: 1. Membership in local businessmen's organizations; 2. Membership in influential out-of-town organizations; 3. Close friends active in Democratic or Republican Party; 4. Close friend or relative in local public office; 5. Wife held a public office; 6. Husband held a public office; 7. Estimate of own role in local government; 8. Estimate of own influence in local government; 9. Estimate of own comprehension of local politics; 10. Estimate of effect of own opinion on local officials; 11. Number of friends or relatives in public office; 12. Number of "top five" influential families named; 13. Personal acquaintance with influential citizens; 14. Retain own lawyer. Items 7 through 10 are adapted from Dahl's findings in a New Haven study,[17] where he argues that those individuals who feel that they exert informal influence over local government, who find local politics comprehensible, and whose opinions matter to local political officials, tend to possess more power than others.

The Assimilation Scale. The scale of assimilation is composed of twelve items, which assess the nature and extent of identification with Germany, its language, and its people: 1. Know anyone who lives in Germany; 2. Number of persons known who live in Germany; 3. Nature of relationship with persons in Germany; 4. Foreign country of preference; 5. Teach children native (German) language of parents; 6. German as a foreign language preference; 7. Extent husband's parents spoke German; 8. Extent wife's parents spoke

[16] Simirenko, *op. cit.*
[17] Robert A. Dahl, *Who Governs?* (New Haven: Yale University Press, 1961), pp. 282–301.

German; 9. Language predominantly spoken at home; 10. Wife reads German books/magazines; 11. Husband reads German books/ magazines; 12. Number of good friends not of German origin.

It was expected that the difference between Turners and non-Turners on the scale of assimilation would be smaller — more than likely insignificant — than on the scale of class, status, or power. Insofar as the Turners no longer form a distinct ethnic community, their possession of Germanic traits or interests should be no greater than that of the non-Turner residents of Germania.

Scale Validity and Reliability. Steps were taken to ensure the validity and reliability of the scales. By *validity* is meant the extent to which the scale scores reflect true differences between the samples in the characteristics measured, rather than random or constant differences. Scale *reliability* is the ability of the instrument to yield equivalent scores on two independent measures of the same individuals.[18]

Validation of the Scales. Partial validity checks were run on the scales of class, status, and power. The validity of these three scales was determined pragmatically on the basis of their ability to distinguish concurrent differences between the class and status positions of known individuals, and to measure the class, status, and power positions of individuals (or families) as evaluated by the Turner and non-Turner respondents. Thus, two kinds of validity tests were made: by the method of known groups, and by the method of jury opinion.[19]

The validity of three scales — class, status, and power — was established. The fourth scale, assimilation, since it measures a relatively unambiguous dimension, the extent of identification with things American, was adjudged valid partly on the strength of its items and partly by comparing the scores of four Germans and four non-Germans who were matched by generation and by class, status, and power scores. The assimilation scale showed a pronounced difference between those respondents who are most German and those who are least German.

Reliability of the Scales. A partial check on the reliability of the scales was made by the test-retest procedure. Two groups, consisting of nine Members[T] and fifteen Founders[T], were contacted in the summer of 1961 and again in the summer of 1962. A measure

[18] Selltiz, *op. cit.*, pp. 154–177.
[19] For a general discussion of pragmatic validity, concurrent validity, and the methods of validating scales, see Selltiz, *op. cit.*, pp. 155–166; and William J. Goode and Paul K. Hatt, *Methods in Social Research* (New York: McGraw-Hill, 1952), pp. 237–239.

of the stability and equivalence of their responses[20] to identical questions on two different occasions is based on four class items: education, value of house, joint income, and net worth. Lack of similarity in responses may be due to changes during the year between interviews and to the difference in the kind of interview. In 1961 questionnaires were mailed to the respondents, whereas a year later personal interviews were conducted.

The degree of association between the two sets of scores is represented by the Spearman rank correlation coefficient.[21] Three coefficients of correlation were established, as indicated in Appendix Table 17.

Appendix Table 17. Correlations of Scale Reliability

Sample	Coefficient of Correlation*
Founders[T] (N = 15)	.94
Members[T] (N = 9)	.67†
Founders[T] and Members[T] (N = 24)	.75

*The correction formula for tied scores was used in computing the coefficient of correlation:

$$r_s = \frac{\Sigma\, x^2 + \Sigma\, y^2 - \Sigma\, d^2}{2\,\sqrt{\Sigma\, x^2\, \Sigma\, y^2}}$$

†One deviant case accounts for this relatively low correlation. When it is eliminated the coefficient of correlation of Members[T] is .98, which brings the total reliability coefficient (Founders[T] and Members[T]) to well above .90.

Though the reliability of all scale items was not checked, the sizable correlations obtained on two applications of four class items — two of which (income and net worth) are usually difficult to discover — the small number of respondents, and the large span of time between alternate measurement procedures all lend weight to the conclusion that the scales are on the whole reliable.

[20] Selltiz, *op. cit.*, pp. 170–176. The stability and equivalence of the scale responses have been ascertained by "the method of *alternative measurement procedures administered at different times.*"

[21] Sidney Siegel, *Nonparametric Statistics for the Behavioral Sciences* (New York: McGraw-Hill, 1956), pp. 202–210.

QUESTIONNAIRE USED IN THE STUDY

1. Code number

2. Age of the wife
   ( ) 1   20-24
   ( ) 2   25-29
   ( ) 3   30-34
   ( ) 4   35-39
   ( ) 5   40-44
   ( ) 6   45-49
   ( ) 7   50-54
   ( ) 8   55-59
   ( ) 9   60-64
   ( ) 10 65 and over
   ( ) R   Deceased

3. Age of the husband, if married
   ( ) 1   20-24
   ( ) 2   25-29
   ( ) 3   30-34
   ( ) 4   35-39
   ( ) 5   40-44
   ( ) 6   45-49
   ( ) 7   50-54
   ( ) 8   55-59
   ( ) 9   60-64
   ( ) 10 65 and over
   ( ) R   Deceased

4. Where was the wife born?
   ( ) 1   Europe
   ( ) 5   United States
         ( ) 1 Germania
         ( ) 5 Outside
               Germania_____

5. Where was the husband born?
   ( ) 1   Europe
   ( ) 5   United States
         ( ) 1 Germania
         ( ) 5 Outside
               Germania_____

6. Wife of German origin
   ( ) 1   No
   ( ) 3   Partly
   ( ) 5   Yes   Ethnic
                  origin_____

7. Husband of German origin
   ( ) 1   No
   ( ) 3   Partly
   ( ) 5   Yes   Ethnic
                  origin_____

8. Ethnic generation of wife
   ( ) 1   Born in Europe
   ( ) 2   Father born in Europe
   ( ) 3   Grandfather born in Europe
   ( ) 4   Fourth or older generation

9. Ethnic generation of husband
   ( ) 1   Born in Europe
   ( ) 2   Father born in Europe
   ( ) 3   Grandfather born in Europe
   ( ) 4   Fourth or older generation

10. Occupation of wife's father
   ( ) 1   Unskilled
   ( ) 2   Skilled
   ( ) 3   Clerical/Sales
   ( ) 4   Managerial/Semi-professional
   ( ) 5   Proprietor/Professional

       Specify:_____

11. Occupation of husband's father
   ( ) 1   Unskilled
   ( ) 2   Skilled
   ( ) 3   Clerical/Sales
   ( ) 4   Managerial/Semi-professional
   ( ) 5   Proprietor/Professional

       Specify:_____

12. Occupation of wife
   ( ) 1   Unskilled (includes housewife)
   ( ) 2   Skilled
   ( ) 3   Clerical/Sales
   ( ) 4   Managerial/Semi-professional
   ( ) 5   Professional

       Specify:_____
       Full time_____ Part time_____

13. Occupation of husband
   ( ) 1   Unskilled
   ( ) 2   Skilled
   ( ) 3   Clerical/Sales
   ( ) 4   Managerial/Semi-professional
   ( ) 5   Proprietor/Professional

       Specify:_____
       Where employed_____
       How long?_____

14. Formal education of wife
   ( ) 1   One to four years

( ) 2 Five to eight years
( ) 3 Nine to twelve years
( ) 4 Thirteen to sixteen years
( ) 5 Graduate school

    Degree held_____
    Graduated from_____
    _____

15. Education of husband
    ( ) 1 One to four years
    ( ) 2 Five to eight years
    ( ) 3 Nine to twelve years
    ( ) 4 Thirteen to sixteen years
    ( ) 5 Graduate school

    Degree held_____
    Graduated from_____
    _____

16. Please give the following information
about your children

Age	Sex	Marital Status	Years Education	Occupation
___	___	___	___	___
___	___	___	___	___
___	___	___	___	___
___	___	___	___	___
___	___	___	___	___
___	___	___	___	___
___	___	___	___	___

(Use other side if necessary)

17. If you have children in high school,
will they attend college?
    ( ) 5 Yes
    ( ) 3 No
    ( ) 1 Undecided

18. If children are under 20, what are
their general occupational aims?
    ( ) 1 Unskilled
    ( ) 2 Skilled
    ( ) 3 Clerical/Sales
    ( ) 4 Managerial/Semi-professional
    ( ) 5 Proprietor-professional

19. Rank the following positions in business in order of preference:
    ( ) 3 Manager, medium-size company
    ( ) 1 Middle management employee,
        large company
    ( ) 5 Proprietor, small company

    What is your basis for this ranking?

_____
_____
_____
_____

_____

20. How many cars owned?
    ( ) 1 None
    ( ) 3 One car
    ( ) 5 Two cars or more ( )

Year and make of each

_____ _____
_____ _____
_____ _____
_____ _____

21. How many miles a year, for business and
pleasure, do you ordinarily travel?
    ( ) 1 Less than 5,000
    ( ) 2 5,000-10,000
    ( ) 3 10,000-20,000
    ( ) 4 20,000-40,000
    ( ) 5 Over 40,000

22. Do you own or have you invested in any
of the following properties?

		Type of property	Amount
( )	1	Boat	_____
( )	2	Airplane	_____
( )	3	Apartment	_____
( )	4	House	_____
( )	5	Store or warehouse	_____
( )	6	Farm or land (acres)	_____
( )	7	Company (mfg., etc.)	_____

23. If house is owned, approximate present
value
    ( ) 1 Under $10,000
    ( ) 2 $10,000 - $15,000
    ( ) 3 $15,000 - $20,000
    ( ) 4 $20,000 - $30,000
    ( ) 5 $30,000 and over
        Value_____
        Taxes paid on property last
        May $_____

24. If rent, what is the monthly rent
    ( ) 1 Under $55
    ( ) 2 $55 - $70
    ( ) 3 $70 - $85
    ( ) 4 $85 - $100
    ( ) 5 $100 and over Rate: $_____

25. ( ) 5 Furnished
    ( ) 1 Unfurnished

26. Type of living quarters
    ( ) 1 Apartment rented
    ( ) 2 Duplex rented
    ( ) 3 Fourplex rented
    ( ) 4 Home rented
    ( ) 5 Home owned

27. If tools and/or equipment are used in
occupation, the value is
    ( ) 1 Under $100
    ( ) 2 $100 - $300
    ( ) 3 $300 - $500
    ( ) 4 $500 - $1,000
    ( ) 5 $1,000 and over Value: $_____

28. Joint income
    ( ) 1 Under $5,000
    ( ) 2 $5,000 - $8,000
    ( ) 3 $8,000 - $10,000
    ( ) 4 $10,000 - $12,000
    ( ) 5 $12,000 and over Amount $_____

29. Ownership of business or other capital
investment, value
    ( ) 1 None
    ( ) 2 Under $10,000
    ( ) 3 $10,000 - $30,000

( ) 4 $30,000 - $50,000
( ) 5 $50,000 and over Amount $_____

30. Who, in your estimation, are the 5 most
wealthy families in Germania (rank in
order of wealth)

1. _____   ( ) 5 Ranked
                          ( ) 1 Not ranked
2. _____

3. _____

4. _____

5. _____

31. Do you know any of them personally?
( ) 5 Yes
( ) 1 No

32. If you (husband or wife) have been to
Europe, for what purpose did you go?
( ) 1 Have not been to Europe
( ) 2 Military service
( ) 3 Education
( ) 4 Visit relatives
( ) 5 Vacation

Other_____

_____
When_____(Years)

33. Have you ever visited Germany (husband
or wife)
( ) 5 Yes
( ) 1 No

When_____(Years)

34. Do you know anyone who lives in Germany
(husband or wife)
( ) 5 Yes
( ) 1 No

35. If so, how many people do you know there?
( ) 1 One person
( ) 3 Two or three
( ) 5 More than three ( )

36. What is their relationship to you?
( ) 1 I hardly know them
( ) 2 Business associates
( ) 3 Casual acquaintances
( ) 4 Good friends
( ) 5 Relatives

_____

37. What are the occupations of the persons
you know in Germany

_____   _____

_____   _____

_____   _____

38. If you were to move to another country,
where would you most prefer to spend
the rest of your life? Rank the following
in order of preference.
( ) 1 France

( ) 2 Scandinavia
( ) 3 Italy
( ) 4 England
( ) 5 Germany

Other most preferred_____

39. Did you teach, or are you going to teach .
your children the native language of
your parents?_____

_____ (specify)
( ) 5 Yes
( ) 1 No

40. Assuming that you know only one language
(English) what foreign language would you
most like to learn? Rank the following
in order of preference.
( ) 1 French
( ) 2 Swedish or Norwegian
( ) 3 German
( ) 4 Russian
( ) 5 Spanish

Other first
preference_____

41. Parents of husband used to speak only
( ) 1 English
( ) 3 English and German
( ) 5 German

Other_____

42. If spoke both English and German, husband learned
( ) 5 German as a child
( ) 3 German and English as a child
( ) 1 English as a child, German later

43. If spoke both English and German, wife
learned
( ) 5 German as a child
( ) 3 German and English as a child
( ) 1 English as a child, German later

44. Parents of wife used to speak (only)
( ) 1 English
( ) 3 English and German
( ) 5 German

Other_____

45. Does the wife read any German newspapers?
( ) 5 Yes
( ) 1 No

46. Does the husband read any German newspapers?
( ) 5 Yes
( ) 1 No

47. Does the wife read any German books or
magazines?
( ) 1 No
( ) 5 Yes: Titles of
             Books   Magazines

_____   _____

_____   _____

_____   _____

48. Does the husband read any German books
or magazines?
( ) 1 No

( ) 5 Yes: Titles of
Books   Magazines

————————— —————————
————————— —————————
————————— —————————

49. Language predominantly spoken at home
(present family)
( ) 1 English
( ) 3 English and German
    Everyone speaks German ( ) 5
    Only parents speak
    German   ( ) 3
    Only grandparents speak
    German   ( ) 1
( ) 5 German
    Spoken by everyone   ( ) 5
    Spoken mostly by parents ( ) 3
    Spoken mostly by grand-
    parents   ( ) 1

50. Type of music favored by wife
( ) 5 Old-time polka
( ) 4 Classical
( ) 3 Semi-classical
( ) 2 Popular hit tunes
( ) 1 Modern jazz and/or American folk

51. Type of music favored by husband
( ) 5 Old-time polka
( ) 4 Classical
( ) 3 Semi-classical
( ) 2 Popular hit tunes
( ) 1 Modern jazz and/or American folk

52. If own a television, how often viewed
during summer
( ) 1 9 to 12 hours a week
( ) 2 6 - 9 hours a week
( ) 3 3 - 6 hours a week
( ) 4 Less than 3 hours a week
( ) 5 Almost never

53. Type of television programs viewed most
by wife
( ) 1 Western, mystery, detective,
    or wrestling
( ) 2 Quiz programs, comedy, or
    musical shows
( ) 3 Theatre (playhouse) or late movies
( ) 4 News and weather, interviews,
    discussions
( ) 5 Concerts and lectures, opera,
    and ballet

    Favorite program_____

54. Type of television programs viewed most
by husband
( ) 1 Western, mystery, detective,
    or wrestling
( ) 2 Quiz programs, comedy, or
    musical shows
( ) 3 Theatre (playhouse) or late movies
( ) 4 News and weather, interviews,
    discussions
( ) 5 Concerts and lectures, opera,
    and ballet

    Favorite program_____

55. House radio-phonograph
( ) 1 None
( ) 2 A.M. radios only
( ) 3 Radio-phonograph

( ) 4 A.M. radio and hi-fi
( ) 4 F.M. radio and a phonograph
( ) 5 F.M. radio and hi-fi

56. Daily paper
( ) 1 None
( ) 2 One paper purchased
( ) 3 One paper delivered
( ) 4 Sunday paper and a daily paper
( ) 5 Sunday paper and 2 daily papers

57. Are you or your husband (wife) familiar
with any of the following papers?
( ) 1 New York Times
( ) 2 Manchester Guardian
( ) 3 Christian Science Monitor
( ) 4 St. Louis Post Dispatch
( ) 5 Washington Post

58. Number of non-German magazines or
periodicals taken
( ) 1 None
( ) 2 One
( ) 3 Two
( ) 4 Three
( ) 5 Four or more: ( )

59. Titles of non-German magazines or
periodicals taken
1. _____

2. _____

3. _____

60. Number of books in the house
( ) 1 Less than 10
( ) 2 10 to 25
( ) 3 25 to 50
( ) 4 50 to 75
( ) 5 More than 75 ( )

61. Type of books in the house
( ) 1 Western, mystery, or science
    fiction paperbacks
( ) 2 Book-of-the-Month or Reader's
    Digest selections
( ) 3 Religious books
( ) 4 Professional
    (Specify)_____
( ) 5 Classics
    Other_____

62. Who generally reads the books in your house?
( ) 1 Children mostly
( ) 3 Parents mostly
( ) 5 Both parents and children

63. Type of movies favored by wife
( ) 1 Western   ( ) 6 Comedy
( ) 2 Adventure ( ) 7 Drama
( ) 3 Mystery/   ( ) 8 Musical
    thriller   ( ) 9 Foreign
( ) 4 Science   ( ) 10 Does not
    fiction   attend
( ) 5 Horror
    pictures

64. Type of movies favored by husband
( ) 1 Western   ( ) 6 Comedy
( ) 2 Adventure ( ) 7 Drama
( ) 3 Mystery/   ( ) 8 Musical
    thriller   ( ) 9 Foreign
( ) 4 Science   ( ) 10 Does not
    fiction   attend
( ) 5 Horror
    pictures

171

65. Attendance at community concerts (husband or wife)
( ) 1 Never
( ) 3 Occasionally: 3 to 5 concerts
a year
( ) 5 Regularly: 6 or more concerts
a year

66. Attendance at theatre plays (husband or wife)
( ) 1 Never
( ) 3 Occasionally: 1 to 3 plays a year
( ) 5 Regularly: 4 or more plays a year

67. Attendance at Twin Cities opera, ballet,
symphony concerts, or plays (husband
or wife)
( ) 1 Never
( ) 3 Occasionally: 3 to 5 times a year
( ) 5 Regularly: 6 or more times a year

68. Membership of wife in clubs and organizations of Germania
( ) 1 Community Concert Society
( ) 3 American Ass'n of University
Women
( ) 5 Great Books Club

69. Wife's membership in out-of-town clubs
or associations
( ) 1 None
( ) 3 1 or 2
( ) 5 More than 2 ( )

Names of associations

_____

_____

70. Husband's membership in out-of-town
clubs or associations
( ) 1 None
( ) 3 1 or 2
( ) 5 More than 2 ( )

Names of associations

_____

_____

71. Wife's total club or organization (local)
membership
( ) 1 None
( ) 3 1 or 2
( ) 5 More than 2 ( )

Names of all clubs and organizations joined

_____

_____

_____

72. Husband's total local club or organization
membership
( ) 1 None
( ) 3 1 or 2
( ) 5 More than 2 ( )

Names of all clubs and organizations joined

_____

_____

172

(Use other side if needed)

73. Does wife hold any position in these local
associations?
( ) 1 No
( ) 5 Yes

74. Does husband hold any position in these
local associations?
( ) 1 No
( ) 3 Sometimes
( ) 5 Always

75. Wife votes in local elections
( ) 1 No
( ) 3 Sometimes
( ) 5 Always
Votes in which elections?
( ) 1 Mayor
( ) 3 School board
( ) 5 City council

76. Is wife active in politics?
( ) 1 No
( ) 5 Yes

77. Husband votes in local elections
( ) 1 No
( ) 3 Sometimes
( ) 5 Always
Votes in which elections?
( ) 1 Mayor
( ) 3 School board
( ) 5 City council

78. Is husband active in politics?
( ) 1 No
( ) 5 Yes

79. Do you have close friends who are active
in either the Democratic or the Republican
Party?
( ) 1 None
( ) 3 One
( ) 5 Two or more ( )

80. Do you have a close friend who is an elected
or appointed official in Germania?
( ) 1 No
( ) 5 Yes

81. Has the wife ever held a public office?
( ) 1 No
( ) 5 Yes_____

82. Has the husband ever held a public office?
( ) 1 No
( ) 5 Yes_____

83. Labor union activity of wife
( ) 1 Does not belong
( ) 3 Belongs, but is not active
( ) 5 Belongs and is active

84. Labor union activity of husband
( ) 1 Does not belong
( ) 3 Belongs, but is not active
( ) 5 Belongs and is active
Office held (if any)_____

85. If you had your choice, would you take a
job paying the same wage in either (husband or wife)?
( ) 1 A private firm, or
( ) 5 A public office

86. How do you feel about local politics?
(Husband or wife) People like myself "have
no say about what the local government does."
( ) 1 Yes
( ) 5 No

87. The only way I can influence local government
is by voting.
( ) 1 Yes
( ) 5 No

88. Local politics and government are too
complicated for me to know what is going on.
( ) 1 Yes
( ) 5 No

89. Local political officials don't care much
what I think.
( ) 1 Yes
( ) 5 No

90. Are any of your friends or relatives now
(or formerly) holding the following public offices?
( ) 1 Mayor
    ( ) 5 Yes
    ( ) 1 No
( ) 2 Chief of Police
    ( ) 5 Yes
    ( ) 1 No
( ) 3 City councilman
    ( ) 5 Yes
    ( ) 1 No
( ) 4 Sheriff
    ( ) 5 Yes
    ( ) 1 No
( ) 5 City manager
    ( ) 5 Yes
    ( ) 1 No

91. Do you know anyone personally whose occupation is (or was)
( ) 1 Doctor or physician
( ) 2 Manufacturer
( ) 3 Banker
( ) 4 Lawyer
( ) 5 Judge

92. Who in your estimation are the 3 more influential citizens of Germania (husband
or wife)

    Name   Position or occupation

1._____ _____

2._____ _____

3._____ _____

93. How many do you (husband or wife) know
personally?
( ) 1 None
( ) 3 One
( ) 4 Two
( ) 5 All three

94. Who in your estimation (husband or wife)
are the 3 most prominent churchmen (Roman
Catholic or Protestant) in Germania?

    Name   Position

1._____ _____

2._____ _____

3._____ _____

95. Do you have your own lawyer?
( ) 5 Yes
( ) 1 No

96. Suppose your best friend was in some kind
of serious trouble in Germania. Who would
you say could help him?

    Name   Position

_____ _____

97. Where is the best place in town to live?
( ) 1 German Street (south)
( ) 2 State and Washington (south)
( ) 3 Klay Addition
( ) 4 Highland Avenue
( ) 5 Summit Avenue

    Other: _____

On what do you base your choice? _____

_____

_____

98. Many of the children and grandchildren of
the first settlers in Germania still live here.
Most towns have "old families" of this nature.
Who are the 5 most widely known old families
in Germania, in order of prominence?

1._____

2._____

3._____

4._____

5._____

99. Do you (husband or wife) know any of them
personally?

( ) 5 Yes
( ) 1 No

100. How well do you know them?
( ) 5 Relatives
( ) 4 Good friends
( ) 3 Casual acquaintances
( ) 2 Business dealings
( ) 1 Scarcely know them

101. Under what circumstances do you usually
associate with them?
( ) 5 Entertain in each other's homes
( ) 4 Go out to dinner and parties
    together
( ) 3 Meet casually while bowling,
    golfing, drinking
( ) 2 Associate for business dealings
( ) 1 Meet in church or while uptown

    Other_____

_____

102. How often on the average do you meet or
get together?
( ) 5 More than twice a month
( ) 3 Once or twice a month
( ) 1 Less than once a month

103. Many people have found that certain types
of marriage do not work out well. Rank the
following "mixed" marriage arrangements
from the most to the least desirable:
( ) 1 Mixed class, wealthy and poor
( ) 2 Mixed nationality, e. g., German
and non-German
( ) 3 Mixed status: old family and out-
sider
( ) 4 Mixed religion, e. g., Roman
Catholic and Protestant
( ) 5 Mixed race, e. g., Negro and White

104. Assuming that you have a daughter who is
about to be married, would you prefer to
see her marry someone from Germania?
( ) 5 Yes
( ) 3 No
( ) 1 Does not matter

105. If a girl were to marry the son of a Germania
family, how would you describe the "best"
sort of marriage she could make?

_____

_____

_____

106. How many good friends do you have who are
not of German origin?
( ) 5 None
( ) 4 One
( ) 3 Two or three
( ) 2 Four or five
( ) 1 Six or more ( )

107. Wife's religion
( ) 1 Roman Catholic
( ) 3 Protestant
( ) 5 Jewish
Other_____

108. Husband's religion
( ) 1 Roman Catholic

( ) 3 Protestant
( ) 5 Jewish
Other_____

109. Assuming that you have children of college
age, what American college or university
would you like to see them attend?
( ) 1 State teachers' college
( ) 2 Small midwestern college
( ) 3 Large midwestern university
( ) 4 Large eastern university
( ) 5 Small "Ivy League" college

Name of school_____

110. Would you prefer that your children study in
Europe?
( ) 5 Yes
( ) 1 No

If so, where in Europe?_____

_____

Why do you have this preference?_____

_____

_____

111. When you eat out, where do you usually go?
( ) 5 Dakota Hotel Dining Room
( ) 4 Eibner's Willamarie Room
( ) 3 Town and Country House
( ) 2 Cat 'n' Fiddle
( ) 1 Beyer's Steak House

Other:_____

Comments_____

_____

_____

174

Bibliography and Index

BIBLIOGRAPHY

Books

Amory, Cleveland, *The Proper Bostonians* (New York: Dutton, 1947).

Anderson, Nels, *The Hobo* (Chicago: University of Chicago Press, 1923).

Arendt, Hannah, *Eichmann in Jerusalem: A Report on the Banality of Evil* (New York: Viking Press, 1963).

——, *The Origins of Totalitarianism*, 2nd ed. (New York: World, 1958).

Baltzell, E. Digby, *Philadelphia Gentlemen* (Glencoe, Ill.: Free Press, 1958).

Beals, Ralph, "Acculturation," in A. L. Kroeber, ed., *Anthropology Today* (Chicago: University of Chicago Press, 1953).

Bell, Daniel, *The End of Ideology* (Glencoe, Ill.: Free Press, 1960).

Bendix, Reinhard, and Seymour Martin Lipset, eds., *Class, Status, and Power: A Reader in Social Stratification* (Glencoe, Ill.: Free Press, 1953).

Bergel, Egon Ernest, *Social Stratification* (New York: McGraw-Hill, 1962).

Bramson, Leon, *The Political Context of Sociology* (Princeton: Princeton University Press, 1961).

Brogan, D. W., *The American Character* (New York: Alfred A. Knopf, 1950).

Chapin, F. Stuart, *Experimental Designs in Sociological Research* (New York: Harper, 1947).

——, *The Measurement of Status by the Use of the Social Status Scale* (Minneapolis: University of Minnesota Press, 1933).

——, *Social Participation Scale*, 1952 ed. (Minneapolis: University of Minnesota Press, 1952).

Dahl, Robert A., *Who Governs?* (New Haven: Yale University Press, 1961).

Dobert, Eitel W., "The Radicals," in *The Forty-Eighters*, A. E. Zucker, ed. (New York: Columbia University Press, 1950).

Faust, Albert Bernhardt, *The German Element in the United States*, Vols. I and II (New York: Steuben Society of America, 1927).

Fritsche, L. A., *History of Brown County, Minnesota*, Vol. I (Indianapolis: B. F. Brown, 1916).

Gerth, Hans, and C. Wright Mills, *Character and Social Structure* (New York: Harcourt, Brace, 1953).

Goode, William J., and Paul K. Hatt, *Methods in Social Research* (New York: McGraw-Hill, 1952).

Gordon, Milton M., *Assimilation in American Life* (New York: Oxford University Press, 1964).

Greenwood, Ernest, *Experimental Sociology* (London: King's Crown Press, 1945).

Hawgood, John A., *The Tragedy of German-America* (London: Putnam, 1940).

Hollingshead, August B., *Elmtown's Youth: The Impact of Social Classes on Adolescence* (New York: John Wiley, 1949).

————, and Frederick C. Redlich, *Social Class and Mental Illness: A Community Study* (New York: John Wiley, 1958).

Hunter, Floyd, *Community Power Structure: A Study of Decision Makers* (Chapel Hill: University of North Carolina Press, 1953).

Johnson, Hildegard Binder, "Adjustment to the United States," in *The Forty-Eighters*, A. E. Zucker, ed. (New York: Columbia University Press, 1950).

Jones, Evan, *The Minnesota: Forgotten River* (New York: Holt, Rinehart, and Winston, 1962).

Kahl, Joseph A., *The American Class Structure* (New York: Holt, Rinehart, and Winston, 1957).

Keucken, Arthur A., *Turnerism Is Americanism* (Detroit: National Executive Committee of the American Turnerbund, 1938).

Kohn, Hans, *The Mind of Germany* (New York: Scribner, 1960).

Kramer, Judith R., and Seymour Leventman, *Children of the Gilded Ghetto* (New Haven: Yale University Press, 1961).

Lasswell, Harold D., and Abraham Kaplan, *Power and Society* (New Haven: Yale University Press, 1950).

Lipset, Seymour Martin, *Political Man* (New York: Doubleday, 1960).

Lovejoy, Arthur O., *Essays in the History of Ideas* (New York: Putnam, 1960).

Lunt, Paul S., *The Social Life of a Modern Community*, Yankee City Series, Vol. I (New Haven: Yale University Press, 1941).

MacIver, Robert M., *Community* (New York: Macmillan, 1917).

————, *Society* (New York: Rinehart, 1937).

Maine, Henry Sumner, *Ancient Law* (New York: Henry Holt, 1906).

Mannheim, Karl, *Essays on the Sociology of Knowledge*, Paul Kecskemeti, trans. (London: Routledge and Kegan Paul, 1952).

Marden, Charles F., *Minorities in American Society* (New York: American Book Co., 1952).

Martindale, Don, *American Social Structure* (New York: Appleton-Century-Crofts, 1960).

————, *American Society* (New York: Van Nostrand, 1960).

————, *Community, Character, and Civilization: Studies in Social Behaviorism* (Glencoe, Ill.: Free Press, 1963).

————, "Prefatory Remarks: The Theory of the City," in Max Weber, *The City*, trans. and ed. by Don Martindale and Gertrud Neuwirth (Glencoe, Ill.: Free Press, 1958).

————, *Institutions, Organizations, and Mass Society* (Boston: Houghton Mifflin, 1966).

————, *Social Life and Cultural Change* (New York: Van Nostrand, 1962).

Mills, C. Wright, *The Power Elite* (New York: Oxford University Press, 1956).

————, "The Sociology of Stratification," in *Power, Politics and People:*

The Collected Essays of C. Wright Mills, Irving Louis Horowitz, ed. (New York: Oxford University Press, 1963).

———, "The Structure of Power in American Society," in *Power, Politics and People: The Collected Essays of C. Wright Mills*, Irving Louis Horowitz, ed. (New York: Oxford University Press, 1963).

———, *White Collar* (New York: Oxford University Press, 1953).

Neill, Edward D., *History of the Minnesota Valley* (Minneapolis: North Star Publishing Co., 1882).

Park, Robert E., Ernest W. Burgess, and Roderick D. McKenzie, *The City* (Chicago: University of Chicago Press, 1925).

Park, Robert E., and Herbert A. Miller, *Old World Traits Transplanted* (New York: Harper, 1921).

Parkes, Henry Bamford, *The American Experience* (New York: Random House, 1959).

Petry, Edward, *The First Fifty Years* (New Ulm: privately printed, trans. by Minnie Loenholt, 1956).

Polanyi, Karl, *The Great Transformation* (New York: Rinehart, 1944).

Polsby, Nelson W., *Community Power and Political Theory* (New Haven: Yale University Press, 1963).

Prahl, Augustus J., "The Turner," in *The Forty-Eighters*, A. E. Zucker, ed. (New York: Columbia University Press, 1950).

Schlinkert, Robert, *The Holy Trinity Church of New Ulm, Minnesota: A Record of 75 Years (1869–1944)*, trans. by Alphonse J. Matt (New Ulm: privately printed, 1944; first printing, 1919).

Schwinn, Alexander, *A History of the Church of St. George of West Newton, Minnesota: 1858–1958* (New Ulm and Mankato: privately printed, 1958).

Selltiz, Claire, *et al.*, *Research Methods in Social Relations* (New York: Holt, Rinehart, and Winston, rev. ed., 1961).

Siegel, Sidney, *Nonparametric Statistics for the Behavioral Sciences* (New York: McGraw-Hill, 1956).

Simirenko, Alex, *Pilgrims, Colonists, and Frontiersmen: An Ethnic Community in Transition* (Glencoe, Ill.: Free Press, 1964).

Sirjamaki, John, *The Sociology of Cities* (New York: Random House, 1964).

Tönnies, Ferdinand, *Community and Society*, trans. by Charles P. Loomis (East Lansing: Michigan State University Press, 1957).

Tyler, Alice Felt, *Freedom's Ferment* (Minneapolis: University of Minnesota Press, 1944).

Vidich, Arthur J., and Joseph Bensman, *Small Town in Mass Society: Class, Power, and Religion in a Rural Community* (Princeton: Princeton University Press, 1944).

Viereck, Peter, *Conservatism Revisited* (New York: Collier Books, rev. ed., 1962).

———, *Meta-Politics: The Roots of the Nazi Mind* (New York: Capricorn Books, rev. ed., 1961).

Warner, W. Lloyd, *American Life: Dream and Reality* (Chicago: University of Chicago Press, rev. ed., 1962).

———, and Paul S. Lunt, *The Social Life of a Modern Community*, Yankee City Series, Vol. I (New Haven: Yale University Press, 1941).

———, Murchia Meeker, and Kenneth Eels, *Social Class in America: A Manual of Procedure for the Measurement of Social Status* (Chicago: Social Research Association, 1949).

Warner, W. Lloyd, and Leo Srole, *The Social Systems of American Ethnic Groups*, Yankee City Series, Vol. III (New Haven: Yale University Press, 1945).

Weber, Max, "Class, Status, Party," in *From Max Weber: Essays in Sociology*, trans. and ed., with an introduction by Hans H. Gerth and C. Wright Mills (New York: Oxford University Press, 1946).

————, "Social Stratification and Class Structure," in Talcott Parsons, *et al.*, eds., *Theories of Society*, Vol. I (Glencoe, Ill.: Free Press, 1961).

————, *The Religion of India*, trans. and edited by Hans H. Gerth and Don Martindale (Glencoe, Ill.: Free Press, 1958).

Weier, Ernst A., *The Work of the Turner Societies* (Indianapolis: American Gymnastic Union, 1919).

Who's Who in Minnesota, Esther Stutheit, ed. (Minneapolis: Minnesota Editorial Association, 1942).

Who's Who in Minnesota, Bernice White, ed. (Waseca, Minn.: Brown Printing Company, 1958).

Whyte, William H., *The Organization Man* (New York: Simon and Schuster, 1956).

Wittke, Carl, *Refugees of Revolution: The German Forty-Eighters in America* (Philadelphia: University of Pennsylvania Press, 1952).

————, *We Who Built America* (Buffalo, N.Y.: Western Reserve Press, 1939).

Zucker, A. E., "Biographical Dictionary of the Forty-Eighters," in *The Forty-Eighters*, A. E. Zucker, ed. (New York: Columbia University Press, 1950).

Articles and Periodicals

Anton, Thomas F., "Power, Pluralism, and Local Politics," *Administrative Science Quarterly*, Vol. VII, No. 4 (March, 1963), pp. 425–457.

Cantril, H., "Identification with Social and Economic Class," *Journal of Abnormal and Social Psychology*, Vol. XLVIII, (January, 1943), pp. 74–80.

Centers, R., "Social Class, Occupation, and Imputed Belief," *American Journal of Sociology*, Vol. LVIII (May, 1953), pp. 543–555.

Gallup, G., and S. Rae, "The Pulse of Democracy: The People of the United States — A Self-Portrait," *Fortune*, February, 1940.

Hatt, Paul K., "Occupation and Social Stratification," *American Journal of Sociology*, Vol. LV (May, 1950), pp. 533–543.

Kahl, Joseph A., and Jerome A. Davis, "A Comparison of Indexes of Socio-Economic Status," *American Sociological Review*, Vol. XX, No. 3 (June, 1955), pp. 317–325.

Lindeman, Eduard C., "Community," *Encyclopedia of the Social Sciences* (New York: Macmillan, 1934).

MacIver, Robert M., "Community," *Encyclopedia of the Social Sciences* (New York: Macmillan, 1934).

Polsby, Nelson W., "Three Problems in the Analysis of Community Power," *American Sociological Review*, Vol. XXIV, No. 6 (December, 1959), pp. 796–803.

Wolfinger, Raymond E., "Reputation and Reality in the Study of 'Community Power,'" *American Sociological Review* Vol. XXV, No. 5 (October, 1960), pp. 636–644.

BIBLIOGRAPHY

Newspapers and Bulletins

Brown County Historical Society Bulletin, New Ulm, 1962.
I. F. Stone's Weekly, Vol. XII, No. 33 (October 5, 1964), pp. 1–4.
New Ulm Daily Journal, June 26, 1962, and August 30, 1962.
New Ulm *Journal Review*, February 14, 1964, and February 14, 1965.
New Ulm Pioneer, 1858, No. 1 (trans. by Mrs. William Durbahn).
New Ulm Review, August 28, 1912.
"The Social Anatomy of an Agricultural Village," Agricultural Experiment Station of the University of Wisconsin, Research Bulletin 34 (Madison, May, 1915).

INDEX

American Association of University Women, 114
American Gymnastic Union, 91. *See also* Gymnastics
American Legion Club, 125
Americanism. *See* Turnerism, American
Arts, patronage of, 110
Assimilation: normal pattern of, 3; Jewish, 12*n*; compared with acculturation, 92*n*; definition, 92*n*, 92–93; aspects of, 93; and friends, 96. *See also* Germany
Assimilation scale: use of, 20; analysis of rejected cases, 153; items of, 165. *See also* Scales
Austin, Horace, 142

Battle of Jena, 28
Beck, Karl, 34
Beats, the, 14*n*. *See also* Status community
Beinhorn, Ferdinand: organizes German colony, 55–56; organizes Chicago Land Verein, 56; supervises town platting, 58; has financial difficulties, 59; meets Pfaender, 59; plans for New Ulm, 59; president of Chicago Land Verein, 59. *See also* Pfaender, William
Belleville, Illinois, 37
Berghold, Alexander, 67
Blatz, Albert, 59

Blatz, Valentine, 59
Books, ownership of, 107–108
Brisbane, Albert, 5
Bull fights, human, 42
Burschenschaften, 27, 29
Businesses, new, 135, 146–147

Cabet, Étienne, 5
Capital worth, comparisons of, 85
Cat, rental of, 64
Catholicism, Roman: and nativism, 16–17, 44; established in Germania, 67; and education, 134, 134*n*; influence in Germania, 134, 135; early reaction to, 134*n*. *See also* Germania
Chicago Land Verein: growth of membership, 56; and land purchase, 56, 59
Cincinnati, Ohio, 46
Cincinnati Turner Society, 6. *See also* Cincinnati Turnverein
Cincinnati Turnverein: and settlement, 6; established, 48; finances colonization, 54, 60; concerned about Germania, 65
Class: definition, 75–76; and status, 75*n*–76*n*, 119, 143; categories of, 76; changing nature of, 76, 76*n*, 77*n*; and education, 78, 162, 162*n*; and stratification, 105; and property, 162–163, 162*n*; subjective evaluation of, 162*n*

Language: proficiency in, 99–101; spoken at home, 101
Language, English: learned at school, 100–101; spoken at home, 100–101
Language, German: preservation of, 99–100; interest in, 100; learned at school, 100–101; spoken at home, 100–101; reading habits, 101
Latin Farmers, 37–38n
Latin settlement, 37–38, 37n–38n
Lawn Club, Germania, 113–114, 113n
Lawyers: influence of, 130–131; Turner, 131–132, 148. *See also* Influence
Leiber, Francis, 34
Lenau, Nikolas, 32
L'Enfant, Pierre Charles, 62
Lincoln, Abraham, 47
Le Sueur, Minnesota, 57, 57n
Lutherans, influence of, 135

McCarthy, Joseph (Sen.), 130n
Magazines, subscriptions to, 107
Mainz Commission, 29
Marriage: intermarriage, 94–95; ideal, 95
Members, definition of, 19
Metternich, Prince Klemens von: opposition to, 27, 34n; supports Turners, 28; warns Prussia, 31; and political repression of liberals, 32
Metternich system, 6, 29
Meyerding, Henry, 65
Middle class, German, 4
Minneapolis, Minnesota, 110
Mississippi River, 57
Mobility, residential, 94n
Mortgage Hill, 119–120
Motion pictures, preferences, 109–110
Müller, Eduard, 49, 49n
Music: preferences, 108–109; as German cultural trait, 109n

Napoleon (*1807*), 28
Napoleonic Wars, 28, 29
National executive committee, policy of, 51–52, 91
National student league: founded by Jahn, 27; opposed by aristocracy, 29
Nationalism, cultural, 26n
Nationalism, German: *19*th-century, 27–28; role of Turners, 28

Nativism: and German-Americans, 43–44; and Catholicism, 44–45; effect on Turners, 47. *See also* Know-Nothing Party
New Ulm, Minnesota: naming of townsite, 58, 62n; early financial difficulties, 59; plan of town, 62; population growth (*1854–1857*), 63; growth in education, 66–67; and Catholicism, 67; anticlerical tendencies, 67; socialistic tendencies, 67. *See also* Germania; Turners, Germania
New Ulm Board of Education, 145n
New Ulm Daily Journal, newspaper, 98
New Ulm Pioneer, newspaper, 64, 66, 134n
Nix, Jacob, 54, 70
Non-Members, definition of, 20
Noyes, John Humphrey, 5

Occupation: of wives' fathers, 79; choice of, 82
Occupational trend: husbands, 79, 80–81; wives, 80; and professionals, 82; and proprietors, 82; decline of entrepreneur, 82
Officeholding, local, 128, 130n
Old Schramm's mill, 64
Owen, Robert, 5

Park Forest, Illinois, 14
Pennsylvania Germans ("Dutch"), 40, 41n
Periodicals, subscriptions to, 107
Pfaender, William: of Cincinnati Turnverein, 53; organizes Turnvereine, 54; promotes colonization, 54, 55; meets Beinhorn, 59; colonization plans, 59–60, 66; finds townsite, 60; negotiates merger, 61; purchases land, 61; president of Land Association, 63, 65; president of Germania, 70; state presidential elector, 142; mentioned, 64. *See also* Beinhorn, Ferdinand
Pfizer, Theodore, 98
Physical education. *See* Gymnastics, Turner
Political activity, 125–126
Political office: holding of, 126; friends